YOU BE YOU

ALWAYS LOVE YOURSELF YOU ARE SPECIAL

WHEN YOU AREN'T THE UNIQUE INDIVIDUAL PERSON YOU ARE, THE WORLD IS MISSING OUT ON SOMETHING GREAT.

YOU ARE THE ONLY YOU

DEVELOPING YOUR TRUE CONFIDENCE WITHIN

Love,

Robyn

CONTENTS

Dedication..

Preface..

Foreword by Erica Young..

Introduction..

D.N.A..

Individuality ....

Comparison...

Influential Voices: Family, Friends and the People Around You ....

Know Your Worth...

Confidence...

Love Yourself ....

You ....

Other Woman's Road to Confidence..

Thank You..

Dedication

This is dedicated to every girl that has ever felt they weren't beautiful. This is dedicated to every person who didn't feel confident in themselves. This is dedicated to every person who has felt they weren't worth fighting for. This is dedicated to every person that feels like they're just like everyone else. This is dedicated to every person that has beat themselves up and has compared themselves to others. This is dedicated to a person that has been told that they are worthless. This is dedicated to any person who isn't confident in their skin. This is dedicated to a person who truly doesn't love themselves. This is dedicated to every hater who wants to stop being a hater.

And this is dedicated to me, Robyn Young, a 13-year-old girl who truly didn't know who she was and didn't love herself for who she was, but realized how amazing she was, and because of that she wrote a book, thank you for realizing that you are the only you.

It was the end of May of the year 2017, and I was at the end of my 6th grade school year. At this point of the end of the year, our teachers pretty much don't care about what we're doing. I was in 2nd period, in one of my favorite and easiest classes "ICT" a computer class. Our amazing teacher Mrs. Waseem "allowed "us to use our phones. So, my two friends Julie and Tiamoy were snap chatting. They both were recording and said, "Team Light-skin" and these two other dark skin girls who were standing next to them said, "Team Dark-skin." After they recorded the video I interrupted and said, "No we're all beautiful." In that time, there was too much of that going on, not only in school, but also on social media. There was too much "dark skins are winning", and "light skins are winning." But I felt that, no we are all winning. I didn't understand why being darker had this bad connotation.

In some people's minds, they have this idea that if you're darker then you're considered uglier, but if you're lighter then you're prettier which is so wrong. But I wanted to research it. I thought there must be a reason and source for this crazy mentality. In my research, I found out that during slavery light-skinned slaves usually worked inside the master's house and the dark-skinned slave worked outside. So, dark skinned slaves were looked down upon simply because their pigmentation was a few shades darker and it was considered bad because in general at that time black was bad. Therefore, if you were light you were a little more acceptable and could work closer to the master's family. After learning this, I realized that this horrible mindset wasn't just an old time mindset but it was something we as the human race struggle with and there was a name for it, colorism. I truly believe that colorism still roams in every street that we walk on. Colorism is discrimination or prejudice towards a person or group of people because of their skin tone. Many people feel that colorism doesn't exist but that is not true and I truly believe that people feel that way because it doesn't impact them personally. But what we must realize is that, just because something doesn't directly impact you, it does not mean it doesn't matter. And for me, I have had countless experiences where colorist remarks were made to me because of the pigment of my skin like when wearing a black shirt someone said, "you are as black as your shirt," or you look like a burnt piece of toast, or I can't see you when we were in the dark during drills at school, or "your pretty for a dark skin,". All of those statements were excruciatingly painful to hear and if you have said or laughed at any of those statements, you are a part of the

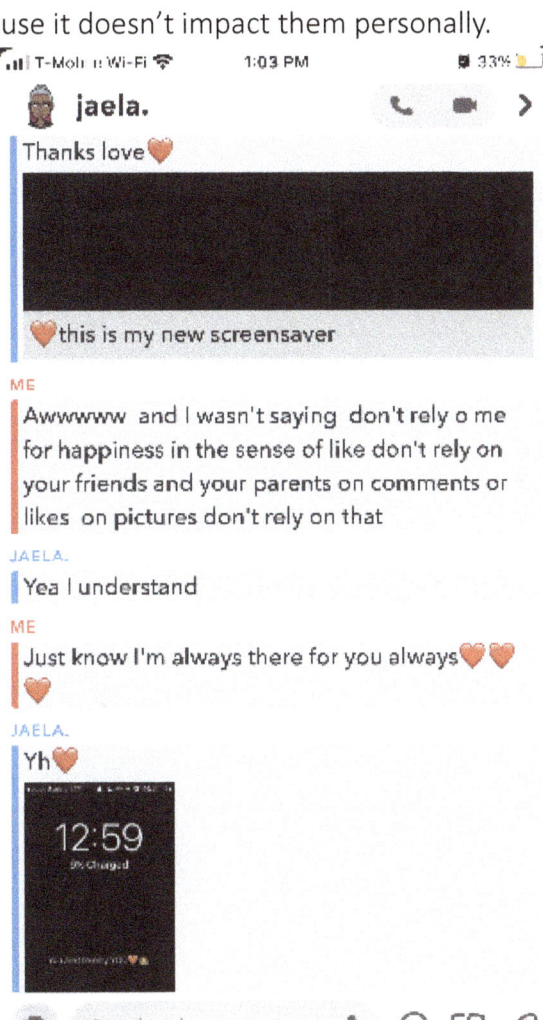

problem. But, it's not too late to be a part of the solution. Just don't say or think those things anymore and realize that all shades are beautiful and should be treated equally. But that realization didn't come so clear to me, I really felt inferior because I was darker. But none of us should ever feel that way because you are not better or worse because of the pigment of your skin.

Your skin is beautiful. It doesn't matter if you have acne or scars or a disease that makes your skin the way it is. Your skin is beautiful.

Now, later that same day when my friends made the snapchat video, I watched a YouTube video where a girl was talking about her experience of being dark skin. The things people said about her were absolutely mortifying and just plain out horrible. After watching the video, I went on a rant on Snapchat about the importance of loving yourself and I really realized in that moment of ranting that that we are all truly amazing. I ended the rant saying, "You Are the Only You." I got like 5 screenshots and I was like, "WOAH!" that's cool. But, the most exciting part was that a girl told me she made "You Are the Only You" her screensaver on her phone, as a constant reminder. Now, when I posted that statement although I was encouraging others to love themselves, I wasn't in a really good place mentally. I do that a lot; help put people back together even when I am falling apart. At this time in my life, I compared myself a lot. I just wasn't happy with who I was. I didn't like who I was. I felt that other people were better than me and that I wasn't enough. So, I began to write. I wrote how I was feeling not knowing that I was writing a book. I wrote how I was feeling, I wrote past experiences. I wrote how I felt. As I wrote I literally let go of all my feelings. Writing was like therapy. Writing helped me say things that I couldn't verbally say out loud.

So, when I started writing how I was feeling I thought maybe this is how other people are feeling or have felt. I wrote this book because I truly want every girl and boy to know that they are special. I want you to know that you are unique and should never feel less than. I want you to know that you are absolutely amazing! So, I began to write to just write and I thought to myself this could actually help someone else other than me. I have always loved writing and my favorite subject in school has always been English. But not only that but I have always had a heart for people and have truly always wanted the people around me to be happy. I thought I could only do that by giving them money, so I aspired to do things that I knew that would give me a lot of money. But I realized what the people around me truly needed wasn't money, but it was love for themselves.

Loving yourself and knowing you are the only you are so important. When writing this book, I was extremely happy because I felt that while you read this you would be happy too. I genuinely love all people, I feel that we as humans are super cool. And if I can inspire one person, I have achieved my purpose. If I inspire you through this book, you may inspire a whole group of other people. Then that same group of people can go inspire others. And then we would have created an inspiration domino effect. I feel that we as people don't think we're special. We feel that we're just some other creation or just blah, but you must realize that you're not. You are special, and you are so unique, and you were created for a purpose.

You are so awesome; do you truly understand that you are the only you? Like literally no one in the entire world is you. Yes, maybe they have your name, but they are not YOU and that is your power. We all know that we are the only us, but we don't act like it at times. If you knew who you were, you would never say the things you say to yourself and allow people to say mean things to you. So that's why I am writing this book to remind and help you confidently know that you truly are the only you.

Foreword

by Erica Young

From the moment Robin entered this side of the universe she began writing her story. Although she is the third of my three beautiful angels, I was as nervous as a first-time mom. After five days had passed, she hadn't opened her eyes and it puzzled me. So, I called my mom and asked her how long after birth do babies open their eyes. My startled mom growled back at me, "What do you mean, babies open their eyes as soon as they are born." Panicking I explained that the baby had not opened her eyes since she was born. Strangely not for a moment did I think my 8.5lb bundle of love-joy was blind, she was too alert. Following my mom's instructions, I took her to the doctor and he reassured me this beautiful, strong, precious treasure was born a survivor.

I endured some challenging ordeals to transport this little champion to the world: she fought her way from beneath fibroids that were as big as her. Robin's pediatrician explained that one of the fibroids rested hard against her face causing severe swelling which caused her eyes to appear closed. She was the most joyful, beautiful baby. Yea! Yea! I know everybody calls their baby beautiful, not the Beckford's. Robin broke the cycle and rewrote the tale of the Young's dynasty. All of our girls were supposed to be boys, well so we thought. My husband and

I were always so certain that we never picked girl names, so all our children were named after birth. She was our last bid, or should I say my last run for "the Junior." Like all my pregnancies my husband chose not to know what gender the baby would be, and my female intuition knew but wouldn't tell him. Because of medical complications I had to have another Cesarean section. I would be put to sleep and the fear of not waking up was beyond anything I had experienced. Finally, after what seemed like I travelled for three days, I felt myself traveling back to earth, and searching for my husband. I must have been calling his name out loud because when I opened my eyes he was there. The first thing I asked him was, "Honey have you seen the baby?" In the most ecstatic voice, he replied, "She is so gorgeous, baby she is better than ten sons." Wow! what a way to welcome a child into the world. We are a family who firmly believes in the power of words. For all of Robin's life

her father has called her gorgeous. Even when she was a tiny little tot in diapers. If he calls her Robin, it means she is in trouble or we may be at some formal setting. As her mom I have had to be a little firmer on her because her dad is still smitten. The saying girls have their dad wrapped around their fingers holds true in the Young's household.

The confident disposition of "My Baba" is directly related to the words and the way she has been treated since she was born. As a Pastor's kid, she has had to share her parents with countless people. She has had to share her home, meals, toys, and especially her mom with other girls. But she has maintained her identity, her biggest pet peeve has been with other people who call me Mommy. Amazingly, I have watched her defend her position on the matter explaining to individuals why it is personal to her. She is a problem solver, and conflict resoluter. She cares deeply for others and expresses her concerns in ways that are truly amazing. Robin reminds us to visit the sick and to take them gifts. At six years old, she worried about a lady who had no husband, "who is she going to spend thanksgiving with she asked?" Did you buy a gift for the Lady who we don't even know her name. She loves deeply, and I am fascinated by her charm and wit. At fourteen going on twenty, Robin has given me such assurance that children will do what you do, and not so much what you say. Her strength of character and determined will was evident at six weeks old when I kept putting her on her side because I was taught that was the safest way to position babies', minutes later, she would reposition herself and when I tried to turn her, she resisted me. From then I knew this child was going to be a force to be reckoned with. I can assure you that no one has the power to reverse the position of her mind. It's been long shaped by the words of her dad..." she is gorgeous and is worth more to me than ten sons carrying on my name."

Her value is in who she is: she is an overcomer, a champion, a conqueror who defied all kinds of medical odds to be here. She fought to be here, and the world will take notice that she has been here. She was born for a purpose. For nine months in my womb I prayed she would carry the glory of God. No wonder she radiates such love and joy. Her confidence to be who she is didn't come from outside forces and influences but from within that little soul that has been anchored in her creator. As I have taught her, whatever you do, keep Christ at the center and you will be all right. He made her beautiful, strong, and powerful. If for any reason she begins to malfunction, she simply needs to go back to her "manufacturer," her creator and he will adjust her, that's called prayer! There is only one Robin Alexia Young: she is my daughter and my critic, I have taken more criticism from her than any other person. From my style to my preaching, even my book. Look out world here comes the indomitable…Lady Robin Young.

Introduction

"You Are the Only You" is not just a book title or a catchy statement, but it is a fact. It is a fact that we are all individuals. It is a scientific fact that we all do not have the same DNA. Growing up, I realized that I wasn't normal. I didn't want to play outside with kids my age. I didn't want to go to the movies with my friends. But, it wasn't because I'm a weird anti-social child, I'm actually the opposite, BUT it was because I felt that I couldn't relate to them. I felt that there was this big bubble of normal people and I was in another big bubble alone. I didn't feel isolated, I felt different. I felt like I always had this burden to help and lead people in the right way and would feel so guilty when making any mistakes. I felt that I was super special which I am, but I honestly thought that I was the only special one, and not special in a good way either. But in a way, that at times I honestly felt better than or worse than, there was never a middle ground. Which I now know is not true or ok, no one is better or worse. You should only compare yourself to who you were yesterday, never to another person. I thought that everyone was normal, and I was just different. So, I began to feel that I should try to be like everyone else, but that failed. For example, cursing. I never like felt pressured to curse, but I sometimes felt weird because I don't do it. Which sometimes made me feel like maybe I should since everyone else does. I felt that all the "normal kids" were doing it so I guess that will make me normal. But there was no turning back and I just couldn't do it. I'm a Christian and I'm a Pastor's kid. My parents have instilled very important values in me, so I know better, so I must do better. Cursing is honestly just overall wrong to me. In the sense it's just so vulgar and just feel that there are so many other ways you can express yourself. But I did, curse when I was 6 (I know bad Robyn) but afterwards I felt so dirty and just felt really guilty. Something within me just knew what I did wasn't a reflection of who I was and it is so important for our actions to be a reflection of our hearts, which may be hard but is so necessary.

Having a very strong conscience is good in my opinion, sometimes it can be good and sometimes it can be annoying because you always feel bad about doing something wrong. For example, I remember my sister Martina found a rolled-up thing of money at the gas station many years ago and she turned it in and we all thought she was stupid. But if she had taken that money I don't think she would've been able to live with herself. Some people have a very strong conscience, and some don't care at all. Like I could never just cuss someone out and walk away. If I did I would then 1 minute after go back and apologize, it would hurt me knowing I hurt someone, you know what I mean.

So anyway, I realized that everyone is special, and everyone is different, I wasn't the only one. We are all different and that's what makes us "the only you's". Being different is good, why would you want to be just like someone else, that is so boring and just lame. I was once told that the funniest looking creation God created was a caterpillar- it's fat, the color is not impressive, and it has prickly things. I personally think that they look gross. I love the saying that goes, but just when the caterpillar thought it was over, she became a beautiful butterfly! When the butterfly is in the cocoon, it is in complete darkness, totally unaware of the beautiful creature that it will be transformed into. Remember, no two butterflies are the same, each one is unique and different in its own ways, and that is what makes it special, just like you and me. At times in life we can get in dark places and we may think we're buried, but perhaps we're just being planted. So, just get prepared to bloom and focus on your flower and the soil that you are planted in. Sometimes, we put so much focus in the flowers around us and its okay to look around but what you should really be focused on is the soil that you are planted so that you will be able to bloom into who you were created to be. But the thing about nature especially flowers, is that they can't bloom until it's their time. So, just wait for your time. Herman Melville once said, "It is better to fail in originality than to succeed in imitation." Which means to me, is that when you try to be like other people you will always fail because you're not being you, you're trying to be them. But when you are fully yourself you will always succeed because you can't fail being you. You can never go wrong when being the only you. Be yourself unapologetically. Sometimes we apologize for being ourselves and maybe laughing too loud, but don't! Be you and be you well. Now, remember there is a time and place for everything, but when is laughing not ok? Wait well at a funeral, but like if they say something funny at the funeral then you can laugh but other than that don't laugh. Being the only you shouldn't be hard, it's actually pretty natural. Just freely be who you are, don't be afraid. I believe one of the main things that stops us from being our true individual selves is the fear of being judged by others and the rejection that may come with that. But, honestly, that is so whack. When you do that, you are literally giving power to that other person and the only person who has power over me is Jesus Christ! So, don't give people power over you, and don't let someone stop you from being you.

Be you. Think like you. Talk like you. Walk like you.

Cue* Walk It Like I Talk It By Migos Be you, and if you're not doing those things like you, honestly anything at literally just someone are think- everyone you are not The legend- Einstein said "what is

you're not doing all, you are copying else. If you ing like else, then thinking. ary Albert it best, right is not

always popular and what is popular is not always right." You set the tone for the rest of your life with what you do today. Every decision you make will affect your future. So, don't copy someone else's decision because their decision will affect them differently from how your decision affects you.

Do your thing and do it unapologetically. Don't pay attention to the haters because well they're haters, why would you pay attention to them? But, know that haters will sometimes be loud, but you have to keep moving forward. By being you, you can make someone happy and possibly inspire change. Fake people aren't relatable, they're envied which is dumb to me because they're fake. Being unapologetically yourself is awesome, don't let anyone tell you different. The word unapologetic is thrown around a lot but I want you to know that it doesn't mean to be rude and to not care about how your actions impact people but it means to be so confident that even when people may disagree with you, you can receive it, process it, and deal with it by either making a change or realizing that what was said wasn't really about you but it was really about their inner insecurities that is being projected upon you.

In the next 8 chapters, you will learn about DNA and how scientifically you are the only you. You will learn how much of an individual you are and how you are adding on to your individuality every day. You will learn about the effects of comparing yourself and how natural it is, but how unhealthy it is. You will learn about influential voices and the importance of those key people in your life. You will learn about the vitality of knowing your worth and knowing what you should and should not take from people. You will learn how to be confident in who you are. You will learn how to love yourself unconditionally. Lastly, you will learn how YOU cannot just say you will do things, but actually do them. I truly believe that by the end of this book that you will truly know that, "You Are the Only You"

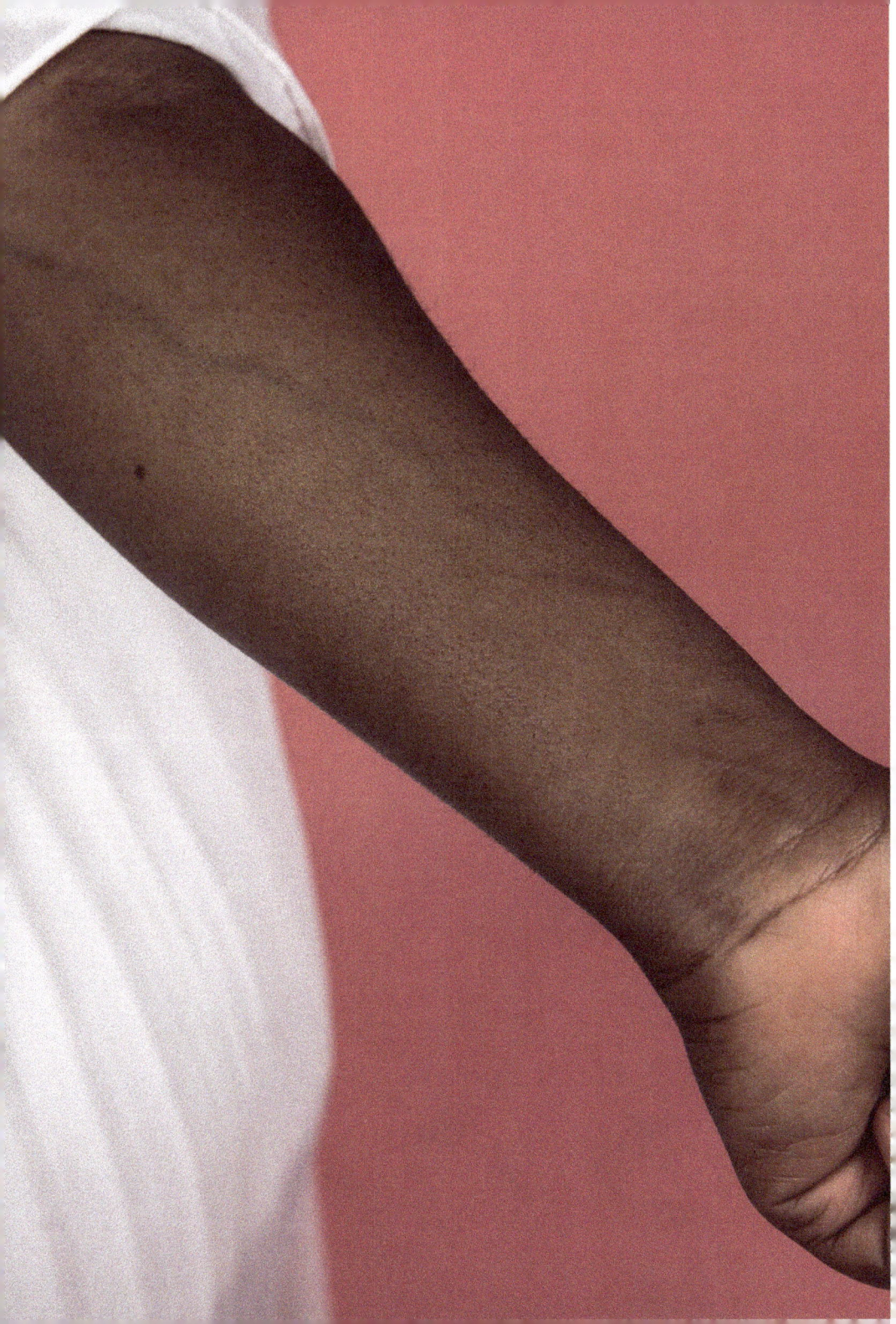

chapter 1

D.N.A

It all starts with DNA. DNA determines who you truly are. The acronym DNA is pretty well known, but do we really know what it means? According to our great friend Google, "The acronym stands for Deoxyribonucleic acid. It is a self-replicating material present in nearly all living organisms as the main constituent of chromosomes. It is the carrier of genetic information, it is the fundamental and distinctive characteristics or qualities of someone or something. So, let's break it down, DNA is a molecule and a molecule is a group of atoms and an atom is the small continent unit of ordinary matter that has the properties of a chemical element. I promise I'm going somewhere with this (lol).

So, remember DNA is a molecule (a bunch of atoms stuck together). It's in the shape of a long spirally ladder and lives in the nucleus. Now you might be thinking, what in God's beautiful world does DNA have to do with the beautiful fact that, "You Are the Only You" well, it actually has everything to do with it. DNA is the one truly important thing that makes me completely different from you. Your DNA defines you more than anything else that exists. Your DNA has a lot to do with your parents as well. My mom has black hair, so I have black hair. My dad is very energetic and excited, so I'm very energetic and excited, okay fine that's not really genetic but still (lol). Your parents have a lot to do with who you are.

YOUR ENVIRONMENT AND THE PEOPLE AROUND YOU ARE VITAL IN DEVELOPING YOU INTO YOU.

My parents are pastors, so therefore, I have been taught and shown a very God-ly way of living, in the sense, that I don't do or say certain things because I have

been taught not to do certain things. The environment you grow in, plays a very important factor in who you are but it is not the end all or be all of who you will become. Now, you might be thinking what does your parents have to do with your DNA? Well a lot, you genetically came from your parents. That whole "situation" happened and now you're here. They have literally given you your DNA if you think about it. You and your parents' DNA are very similar if you checked it out. Your parents are very much a part of you, so be happy if you have good ones (lol), and if you don't at least you have them in your life and they didn't drop you on the side of the road.

Bill Gates once said, "DNA is like a computer program but far, far more advanced than any software ever created," and that statement is so true. According to Sharon Brigges," Humans are 99.9% identical and what makes us different is a measly 0.01% of our genome. This may seem insignificant. But what these facts don't show or point out is that the human genome is made up of three billion base pairs, which means that 0.01% is still equal to three billion base pairs. In those three billion base pair lie differences that give you red hair instead of black hair or green eyes instead of blue eyes. That small 0.01% determines that you could be short or tall. Brigges had the best analogy for DNA that stated, "Imagine that your DNA is a car. There are certain obvious variants you can have: blue or white, two –door or four doors, convertible or sedan. These differences represent that 0.01%. The other 99.9% is the engine, the seats, the steering wheel, and the tires, those parts must be there for the car to work." So, although that 0.01% doesn't seem that significant, IT REALLY IS! This 0.01% determines that our hair is different, and our skin color is different.

Your DNA does contribute to your personality, but it is not based on it entirely. Genes are not completely responsible for our personality. Your environment has a lot more to do with your personality than your genes. Where we live and the culture we have grown up in truly makes a mark on our personality. I was talking to one of my friends Jaaqaun and he was telling me that he's from Paterson, New Jersey. He said people are pretty aggressive. They are very selective on who they trust and will allow around their private space. Because of the crime in the region he said, "You can't be scary, or people will see you as prey. Also, your own friends will steal from you and you don't even know it." This demonstrates how your environment impacts who you are. Jaaquan is a little more aggressive than others because he's lived in Paterson, New Jersey, which makes sense. Think of all the places in the world. Now, consider how many different types of people there must be considering Jaaquan. There are around 7 billion people in the entire world and each person on this planet is very different. It is important to know that we have been placed and made just they we are to impact the people around us and we also have to know that we are impacted by the places we reside and the people we reside with. The personalities and the attiudes we have are all reflections of so many components and are environment is a big one. A woman named Nyanbembo once said, " the environemt we live in naturally influences our personality but our personality can influence our environment as well."

Our personality is a complex trait, which is a trait defined by many different genetic and environmental traits as defined by Study.com. Genetic traits and environmental traits give you your personality. We are all so different and unique in so many ways. We are truly one of a kind and you know what they say about things that are one of a kind, they are invaluable.

So again, the scientific acronym for DNA is deoxyribonucleic acid, but I want to

THE PERSONALITIES AND THE ATTIUDES WE HAVE ARE ALL REFLECTIONS OF SO MANY COMPONENTS AND ARE ENVIRONMENT IS A BIG ONE.

give you an acronym that you can use daily, sort of a new way to think of DNA. The acronym that I want you to use is **Daily Necessary Attitudes**. I'm going to give you 4 vital attitudes that you should have to be the best version of yourself.

1. BE POSITIVE

The word positive means in the simplest sense, according to our great friend Google, "Good or the opposite of negative. Now the complicated meaning as defined by Webster Merriam is, "Consisting in or characterized by the presence or possession of features or qualities rather than their absence." You're glad I read the simple meaning aren't you (lol). But seriously, I feel that the complicated definition means, looking at the glass half full rather than half empty. It can be easier at times to look at life in a negative perspective. But, honestly there are way more positives in life than negatives. I challenge you right now to put this book down, and think about 5 positive things that happened in your day today. Now, there is a chance you struggled or got it done in a breeze but I bet if I asked you 5 negative things, you could name them with no problem but to me, that is an issue because I want both you and I to have a mentality of gratitude.

In life, we can complain and be unhappy about a situation not going our way and don't get me wrong it happens. Life is full of obstacles and ups and downs, but honestly, really try to be positive. Look for something positive in each day, even if some days you have to look harder, it's always there! Train your mind to see the good in everything. When you feel you're about to be negative stop yourself and really think about it, life is so great. I'm literally breathing right now, come on (insert YOUR name). People ask me all the time, how I am so positive all the time and my response is always, I just think about how great life is and the fact that I am literally breathing right now. My sister Akeima usually gives me a look every time I'm being ungrateful or negative, which keeps me in check. If the ice cream machine isn't working at your favorite fast food restaurant and you really wanted ice cream think about it, maybe if it was working, a roach would've crawled in it and then you would've eaten a roach. Positivity is a choice!

I'm going to give you a situation. I will give you the negative response and you're going to think about the positive response.

Situation: Someone says something rude or mean to you.

Negative Response: Respond with another mean statement and possibly get in a physical and/or verbal altercation.

Positive Response: (think about it) What you possibly thought? ~ Breathe and play your favorite music and think about it, that person could've had just lost their mom from breast cancer or they are just being annoying for no reason. But regardless of the reason, you are not going to allow someone to have you step out of character and you will not stoop down to their level.

Situation: Mom yells at you to wash the dishes or you are yelled at to do something

Negative Response: yell and say "I don't want to" with an attitude and then probably get yelled back at

Positive Response: (think about it)

What you possibly thought? ~ Say, "yes Mommy" and think about it she did carry you for like 9 months and then pushed you out. If the person is not your mom, respond in love because yelling back in forth is draining and honestly isn't worth the lovely breath in your body.

Always remember, the happiness of your life depends on the quality of your thoughts. Realize a negative mind will never give you a positive life.

2. DON'T BE MEAN

Katie Holmes once said, "You can be pretty, talented, and smart but no one will remember any of those things if you're mean." If you're mean to people, what are you really doing? Like seriously, why do you think that you have the right to hurt someone's feelings? Realize, when people say bad things about you it's only because they are just insecure within themselves. Now we hear that statement a lot but let's talk about that insecure person. You are insecure, I'm sorry. But you don't have the right to make someone feel bad because you feel bad about yourself. Honestly, if you are really insecure and unhappy with yourself, my advice is that you write down exactly how you're feeling and talk to yourself. Tell yourself or talk to someone about how you're feeling. I talk to myself and I have a relationship with myself and I think that everyone should have one too.

GET TO KNOW WHO YOU TRULY ARE AND BE HONEST WITH HOW YOU ARE FEELING AND FIND OUT THE WHY OF YOUR EMOTIONS

Now, I know that probably sounds crazy, but I think it is very important. Get to know who you truly are and be honest with how you are feeling and find out the why of your emotions. Let how you are feeling be heard, communicate, even if it's just with yourself. But don't be mean. There is always a source when someone has self-hatred, anger, or bitterness; it doesn't just come out of nowhere. It might feel that way but that's not the case. No one is just born a mean person, it is either taught or learned. Find the source of your negative and mean attitude because there is one. Think about what triggers that reaction. But ultimately, you have to make the decision on how YOU are going to live and behave for the rest of your life.

Overall, just don't be mean, it's not adding to anyone's life especially not yours. Remember when someone is mean to you it has nothing to do with you but everything to do with them. If you should ever find yourself the victim of other people's bitterness, jealousy, lies, and insecurities don't be mad remember things could be worse, YOU COULD BE THEM!

We constantly see in the media world and in our regular world people are mean to other people. They are always calling other people out of their names. Girls call each other horrible and derogatory names and they think it's cute, but it's not. Especially in our world today, where the President of the United States calls NFL players mean names without a second thought. We must do better. Just because someone doesn't do something like you, doesn't mean you should be mean or judgmental toward them. You have every right in the sense of freedom of speech, but is that nice? Just because something is legal or accepted, it doesn't make it rght. You have the right to your opinion, but express your opinion with love and respect. But realize some words are just unkind and should not be said.

But, again just don't be mean. I've said this statement a lot in the last couple of pages because I really want you to get it in your head that, being mean is not cool and it's not okay. You don't want to be remembered as a mean girl. If you do and if you find satisfaction in other people's pain, you really have a problem, but that's another story. Don't be that one negative person. I remember I wore this really pretty dress on Sunday to church many years ago and I was getting so many compliments from everyone and I obviously felt good. But I was standing up by this chair by another girl nearby, and she said, "You could've tied the string and you're dress I guess is pretty (under her breathe in a bad attitude) and it didn't really hurt me, but it again showed me this girl's true colors. There will always be that one negative person but don't be that one person and if enough of us choose to not be that one negative person, then the world would be such a more positive place. No one likes a mean girl and if they do, it's only for a matter of time until they're all alone and have to come face-to-face with the person they have become. And I want to be clear that sometimes people really want to help and offer advice but you can do it in love, if that person really wanted to help me fix the dress they would have said it in love but they didn't and that's okay because it is again a reflection of who they truly are.

3. BE EFFICIENT

Again, according to our great friend Google, the word efficient means, "achieving maximum productivity with minimum wasted effort or expense." John Brown once said, "They laughed at my dreams, now I laugh at their lifestyle." I want to be able to say that one day, but only if I work efficiently. One really important skill that both of my sisters have taught me is go, go, go, go, go and go and always follow your dreams. They've taught me not to waste time and don't just do it, but do it with all your energy and passion. They've also said," don't ever let anyone tell you, you can't achieve something because your energy is the only thing that determines that". Efficient people will always will succeed.

My dad graduated from college recently with honors, and he didn't just get a degree, but he worked hard for it. He has taught me to give 100% of your energy in everything you do, don't do anything half way, not even wash the dishes. Thanks Daddy, love you lots! Being efficient is similar to working hard, but with more passion and drive involved. Be efficient with your time. Do something you are proud of and confident about. In being efficient you can become a leader, not just at school or at work, but in life in general. Being a leader is deeper than just being in charge of something but being a true leader is not just being responsible for the people around you but being responsible for yourself and the actions and decisions you make. More importantly, efficiency truly helps you to develop into a better person. As a leader and as truly anyone, you must be self- aware. It is important to know that with beng efficent you must be self aware and be mindful of the things that you are doing. It is important to note that the most important person doesn't survive but honestly the most efficient person. Live every moment with wisdom and efficiency. Remember the goal is to become and accomplish your purpose on this earth, so why not do with confidence and do it efficiently?

4. BE GENUINE

Now when writing this I felt that I contradicted myself because I'm telling you to be genuine which is like the opposite of being genuine. But just hear me out. The definition of genuine according to our great friend Google is, "what something is said to be, authentic'." We live in a society where looking cool in pictures on social media has become more important than being a genuinely cool person, as long as it looks believable in the picture. But, being genuine is so important, not only because people usually know when you are, but because faking how you feel is unhealthy. The statement, "fake it till you make it", is very popular. But I personally have never been a fan. I believe faking it till you make it is unhealthy. I once heard someone say in the contrary, **face** it till you make it, which meant to me, face the situation heads on and figure it out rather than pretend like you can handle something when you need help because needing help is okay. I believe you should feel every emotion you have, be genuine with how you feel, and you shouldn't have to fake anything. I say this because I did that same thing for a very long time, just going through the motions. Going to church every Sunday, going to school, praying that same 1-minute prayer. But then I realized I didn't want to just exist, I wanted to live, I didn't want to fake it till I made it. I wanted to say how I felt and be genuine. Now let's say you don't like someone's shoes that doesn't mean you should go up to them and say, "I don't like your shoes", because you're being genuine. But, it means if everyone is complimenting them that doesn't automatically mean you have to as well. Don't feel that if everyone in the room likes pudding, you have to like pudding. There is nothing wrong with you and there is nothing wrong with the pudding, you two just don't get along and that is okay, be genuine to how you feel.

I read this amazing book called "How to Be a Bawse" by Lilly Singh and in her spectacular chapter called, "Say What You Mean" she talked about how we as people are so politically correct. She used the example, like when someone asks, "how are you?" people automatically say good, but are you usually? You don't have to say good, you can say spectacular or you can say not that good, but be genuine with your answer. Be genuine with everything you say and do. Genuinely tell someone you love them, genuinely pray to God, and genuinely talk to people! Don't be robotic, robots are metal, and metal is hard and you don't want to be hard. Give your 100% genuine energy in everything you say and do, and you will truly be the best you.

I promise, if you have these 4 DNA's (Daily Necessary Attitudes) you will be the best only you possible and you will just be a better person overall. At the end of the day, we are still more similar than we are different. But we are just beginning to understand how important and vital are differences are.

chapter 2

INDIVIDUALITY

I stare at myself in the mirror, I see one bump, and two bumps and there goes another. In that moment, it literally feels like the end of the world. It's not just because I'm young and a teenager, but like everyone goes through this, I think. I think to myself, "everyone at school is going to see it, my life is over. " Then, I think again and then consider, "well it's not that bad and I don't care what they think anyway."

I feel that every single one of us has similar conversations like these with ourselves, and it's not that you're crazy, but it happens. Sometimes our skin looks really good and sometimes it looks pretty bad. But when you think about it no one has that same exact bump on their face or no one has that exact nose shape, or no one has that same un-even eyebrow. No one is like you because you are an individual. When I asked Siri, what does individuality mean she tells me, "the quality or character of a particular person or thing that distinguishes them from others of the same kind, especially when strongly marked. And the more formal meaning according to The Webster Merriam is," of relating to, or distinctively associated with an individual or existing as a distinct entirety." Now being an individual is super lit (lit means cool, for you older folks, lol). Seriously, think about it, nobody walks like you, or talks like you or eats like you, there are definitely similarities, but not exactly like you. Many people have told me I look like my older sister Martina. Although that is completely true, we still are two completely different individuals.

Sometimes we feel that we lose our individual selves because we are constantly being compared. But you can't lose your individuality. The fact that you're breathing and alive, makes you an individual because of the way you are doing it. You can lose your identity, but you will never lose your individuality. You can lose your identity from being in an unhealthy relationship, being in a traumatic situation, or even just living life going through the motions. Now you might feel that you are losing your identity, but you will never ever lose your individuality. For example, Kim Kardashian West and Kylie Jenner are always being compared not only because they're related, but also because they have many similarities. They both have makeup lines, they both have daughters, and they both are super rich. Being your true individual self can be very hard, either because you're constantly being compared or because of the many distractions in the world. All around us we are bombarded by noise that can hinder us from focusing on our quest of becoming our best. I watched a documentary called *Individuality*. One of the many people in the video said something so profound that I would like to share with you. He said, "Basically in every which way I'm different from someone. Although we can share similar interest or similar cultural beliefs or something, just the fact that maybe I saw one movie that someone hasn't already automatically makes me different because I have certain knowledge another person doesn't." That is beyond powerful. The singular fact that you know something that I don't makes you more of an individual than you already were. Why? Because I know something that you don't! Our minds contribute to our individuality. The knowledge we have or don't have makes us individuals. There are trillions of variables in this life that affect who a person is, so basically from birth I'm different from everybody.

I've realized that it can sometimes be easier to follow the crowd rather than stand up and lead. But why is that? It's because of fear. Now if you think about it, we weren't born with fear. The Bible says in 2 Timothy 1:7 in the KJV, "For God has not given us the spirit of fear, but of power and of love and of a sound mind". I know without a doubt this is true. Because think about it, parents often tell their children not to touch the hot stove when they're younger because they don't want them to get hurt, but they still do. Before that command the child was never fearful of the stove. Now, as you can probably tell that child wasn't fearful of the stove, they were simply curious. We weren't born with fear. But as we grow and gain consciousness, we become scared of things and of the world around us. I really believe that we are taught fear. Fear isn't innate within us, it is ultimately just issues in our hearts, when we fear we are allowing the future to ultimately impact our present in a negative manner. The reality is we must understand that fear kills more dreams than failure ever could. My teacher always used to say you miss 100% of the shots you never take. A man named George Addair once said, "Realize everything you want is on the other side of fear." And that is truly completely facts, we can only fully express our true selves when we remove the burden of fear that is resting on our shoulders. We really have to let go of fear because fear will lead to many other things and surprisingly enough judgement is one of those things. We judge what we fear and are too proud to understand.

Sometimes us as humans, we judge others' individuality. This judgment is rarely because we're mean or bad spirited. But because we are so accustomed to our way of living we believe anything outside of what we think is wrong. Another reason why we judge people's individuality is because we are unwilling to learn new things. At times we are stuck in our ways and decide not to have an open mind. I am saying have an open mind even if you do not agree, you might learn something. I could really disagree with what you are saying, but out of respect I will listen. Try to see the other person's perspective even if you don't agree. I have been in countless conversations with people that I know literally stands for everything contrary to what I am saying but out of love and respect, I hear them out because I would want them to hear me out. And this is not to say to sit through toxic and detrimental conversations, you should definitely use your own discernment. But, I believe we are so easy to walk away from conversations simply because the person has a different perspective. And yes some people feel hopeless but all you can and should do is try. Being ignorant is not really the issue but staying ignorant is the issue. Being cognizant of the issues in our world and just in general is so important. There are so many ways to be informed, you have no excuse. The legendary Nelson Mandela once said, "The more informed you are, the less arrogant and aggressive you are." Ignorant people are usually angry and defensive, and I don't think you want to be angry or defensive all the time. I really believe that sometimes anger and aggression truly stems from insecurity. When someone feels that there character has been attacked they usually respond with aggression and a spirt of defensiveness and if you look at it from a very surface level, you'll think, "OH they are just having a bad day". But more than less of the time, it really is coming from there insecurities within and not just that but it is also because of ignorance. When you are ignorant of what triggers you or of who you are, it opens many doors of frustration, anger, jealousy, comparison, and ultimately sadness. When you aren't knowledgeable of what makes you do or say the things you do, you are missing a huge part of your individuality. We must realize that knowledge in all forms is power. So, when you have knowledge about people, cultures, yourself, and life in general you will not judge people's individuality, you will actually appreciate it.

I am glad we are all different and individuals. Imagine if we weren't, that would be so boring. We would feel like we were all robots and who wants to be a robot? So, pretty much do your best to not be an ignorant person, be as knowledgeable as you can be. You aren't going to know everything or every word in the dictionary but it is important for you to speak and act with knowledge. I saw a post made by @the.foreword on Instagram the other day, and it was encouraging people to get comfortable saying these 4 things. 1. Thanks for correcting me, I didn't realize that. 2. I hadn't thought of it like that. I understand now. 3. I was wrong about that, and I've changed my mind. And 4 my favorite one says, I should do more research before I argue that point. I loved all of those statements because there is truly no shame in being wrong, but only refusing to learn. When you aren't informed on something, it is okay not to speak on it until you are more informed and if not just be careful with what you're saying. It is so important for people to be understanding because we are all growing and learning, regardless of how old or young we are. People should feel comfortable being themselves, except if there doing detrimental drugs and illegal harmful stuff, but you get what I'm saying. You truly are the Only You and that is a beautiful thing.

At the end of the day people will try to tell you what to look like, talk like, and be like, but you must realize that everyone has their own individual calling and purpose. So, just because theirs doesn't look like yours, it doesn't mean they are doing the wrong thing, it just means that they are living out their true individual selves. And you should do the same. Rather than bothering them and trying to live up to the expectations of others, focus on developing your individuality. If everyone was the same, imagine how boring life would be. If you think about it life is extremely fragile and although I don't like thinking about it, we could all die in like 8 seconds. So why spend any minute of your beautiful life wanting to be other people when you can be the most spectacular individual you were created to be and that you deep down truly are.

The word individual is honestly very hard to define because there are so many perspectives on the word. I have told you Siri's definition and I have told you Mr. Webster's definition, but here is mine. Individuality: literally everything about you that makes you, what makes you different from the rest. Don't get me wrong you're going to have similarities with many people, but that doesn't make you any less of an individual. Realize that we are all already individuals, adding to our individuality every day. Daily we are changing, growing, and learning new things. We learn new things every day without realizing it. You watching that movie yesterday has made you even more of an individual than you already are and another person isn't any less of an individual because they didn't watch that movie. The simple fact that I know something you don't makes me even more different. By the way different is good. Why would you like to be like everyone else? That's basic and we don't want to be basic. Remember if you walk in the footprints of others, you will never ever make your own.

YOU CAN LOSE YOUR IDENTITY, BUT YOU WILL NEVER LOSE YOUR INDIVIDUALITY

chapter 3

COMPARISON

All my life I have been loved. My parents are so spectacularly amazing. My daddy loves me with all of his heart; he tells me when he likes my hair, and when he likes my outfit, and is extremely supportive of everything that I do. My name in his phone is Gorgeous, so that says it all. My Mommy also loves me with all of her heart, she always makes sure I'm fed (which is super important) and tells me the truth even when I don't want to hear it (which is very necessary), and she is always there when I need to talk. My sisters are my best friends. They constantly check on me and tell me they love me, and they really want me to succeed. Akeima has made me such a great person, her advice is priceless, and she is extremely wise. Martina has dealt with my constant calls on a daily basis and has shown me the road to a successful life. My brother in law Javaun has helped me realize that I don't need a filter to be beautiful; he is extremely encouraging and supportive of all my dreams. My Aunty Jay is always a phone call away and I know I'm her favorite out of the three of us. My church family loves me and is extremely involved in my day to day life. My friends mean the world to me and are so encouraging to me and all that I do. I say all of that not to brag but to say I have literal confidence boosters around me 24/7. You know those energy drinks that people drink for energy? My family and friends are my energy drinks. I have people that give me constant confidence. I have never really had low self-esteem, but I did and do sometimes compare myself.

I have heard that if you compare yourself to others you have low self-esteem and that can be true, but not in my case. At times I would crazily enough, compare myself to myself. That sounds crazy, right? But it's like if I had a great day on Thursday, but then I have a horrible day Friday, I get annoyed with myself. I would beat myself about it, because well, I should've done better than yesterday. I will say, I at times can be very hard on myself. I want a lot out of life, which is okay. But there are levels to it. Trying to get better daily is healthy, but beating yourself up is extremely detrimental to becoming the best you possible. I had to realize that. Progression is what most people want out of life but at what cost? It is important to want to better ourselves but is it worth risking our peace of mind? Everyone has different views on what working hard is and what working too hard is and ultimately you are the only who can decide that for yourself. So, maybe writing a 10 page paper is easy and super fun for me, but for you that could literally be death. But then again, you could do a math worksheet in 10 minutes and it take me 10 hours. Everyone is different and you just have to do what ultimately feels right and aligns with your morals. I was talking to my sister Martina and she was saying for her, self-care is drinking tea and I laughed but realized how simple but profound what she said was. For you, maybe drinking tea is an everyday thing but for her it's not, and maybe for her getting a massage every week is a must but for you that only happens on holidays and that is A-Okay. But, sometimes we don't think it's A- okay and we fall into the trap of comparison. Comparing what works for you and what works for someone else is unhealthy and doesn't push you into becoming the best version of yourself.

Growing up in this world of technology, it can at times be hard for you to be happy with who you are and hard for you not to compare yourself. In December of 2016, I got my first phone with service. I had a phone previously, but it didn't have service. (lol) The first app I downloaded was Snapchat which was really cool at the time. I added people I knew, posted cute selfies, posted Sunday outfits, rants on loving yourself, and inspi-

COMPARING WHAT WORKS FOR YOU AND WHAT WORKS FOR SOMEONE ELSE IS UNHEALTHY AND DOESN'T PUSH YOU INTO BECOMING THE BEST VERSION OF YOURSELF BUT A BETTER VERISON OF THEM .

rational quotes. That all sound like clean fun, right? Well, it was until I started watching other people's snaps and I would go into a deep hole of comparing myself to others. I would compare dumb stuff like my hair, or shoes, or nails, or even eyebrows. I would think 'why is her hair so shiny", or "how are her teeth so straight", or "how are her selfies so cute "and "how does she have 180 likes and I only have 99 likes." Imagine doing that every day. Like I said I didn't think I was ugly, but I thought I wasn't as pretty compared to others. When you are not confident within yourself you become insecure and when you are insecure you constantly feel like a victim or attacked. For example, if I posted on Snapchat the statement people who wear wigs are dumb (btw I would never say that). If you are a confident person who wears wings that won't phase you because you know you're not dumb, so what I have to say is irrelevant to you. But, if you are an insecure person who wears wigs that will highly affect and offend you. You might even feel personally attacked. But, maybe I was just talking about my friend Gloria's wigs as a joke. Or here is another example, which I personally have gone through. I post a lot on Snapchat and sometimes people have told me that I post too much, or they say that they skip through my snaps. My response is normally, well unfollow me and or okay. My confidence in who I am and what I post doesn't allow their comments to affect me. Why? Because I know what I post is inspirational and can be beneficial to people's lives. It would be different if I was posting foolishness, but I'm not. When you are not confident in yourself you feel that the world is out to get you but in actuality, it really is not.

One of my many aspirations in life is to be a successful actress. When I would see other young actors succeeding, I would compare myself to them. Although, I should be happy for them, I honestly wasn't at the time. I'll be really honest, I remember when Marsai Martin announced that she wrote, was starring in, and was producing her own film entitled, "Little". I honestly was jealous and was thinking, "why isn't that me or why couldn't that be me? Which are all not nice things to think.

I was definitely happy for her but deep down envious of what she had accomplished at the same age as me. And see the thing is, the reason I even thought those things was deep down because of insecurity, because

Photo Source: imdb.com

I knew deep down that I was capable of being successful in mine own way but wasn't. I was more jealous because she was where I only dreamed of being. So, it was more about me and my insecurity than her and her success. Realize that envying someone and their success won't bring you any closer to your own success. You also have to realize that every minute you spend wishing you had someone else's life, you are wasting a minute of your own that you could've been spending on focusing on your own. Tamera Mowry Housley once said, "Another woman's win isn't your loss." That is so true. I had to realize that we can all win together. If your friend is succeeding don't be jealous or upset, but be happy, because when you succeed you want them to support you as well. But also, being a hater is not nice and you should be nice. But, really and truly it's just the right thing to do. Treat people how you want to be treated. But, honestly not just that but be intentional with your thoughts because you can easily think bad about people in your mind but then speak good with your mouth. So, it is very important to make sure that you are checking yourself and constantly being self-aware. Because no one knew that I was jealous of Marsai at that time, I posted about her on Instagram and talked good about her to people but in my mind and heart I was jealous. And that moment truly changed me because I had to really be real with myself and do some soul searching on why I was having the thoughts I was having. Now, you may be thinking, are you still jelly of Marsai and the answer is a big NO! I am very proud of her and all her success. I am so inspired by her and she motivates me in so many ways. She inspires me to follow my dreams because when I see her, I see me and she's shown me that no matter your age, you can accomplish your dreams. So, don't just treat people how you wanted to be treated with your words but do it with your heart as well. All in all, why be mad, sad, hateful, and envious when you could be happy, grateful, and inspired?

But back to the apps. After I downloaded Snapchat, I then downloaded Instagram. I would scroll, like, and comment. But, then I would again compare people's captions to my captions or compare their hair to my hair. Social media can be a blessing and a curse, it's just how you use it. Social media can help you or tear you down. I would again compare my life to people's pictures and everything in between. I then realized how unhealthy it was, and I knew I had to do something about this. I needed to change. So, here's a tip that definitely helped me, take a break, go on a fast. Don't go on social media for like 3 days or a week or even 21 days. However long you think is good for you. This stopped me from being so dependent on social media for happiness and I found my true happiness in God, well later on. I say later on because it didn't happen overnight and that's okay.

Moreover, the thing is comparing yourself is so easy because, well it just is, you're human. If Sabrina has a purse I want, instead of me complimenting it and moving on with my life, I compare myself and just become unhappy with myself over Sabrina's purse, which sounds crazy right? But, sometimes you get to that place. At times, us as a society, we can find ourselves wanting things that were not destined for us. I have met so many people who are in single-parent homes. Honestly, some are glad that they were because they learned so much from the experience. Now me on the other hand I can learn from both of my parents being in my life. I really believe life happens the way it is supposed to. I promise you, you will experience every experience you were created to experience. Your life has already been planned by God, all you have to do is follow his will. I used to rush so many things in life because I was inpatient but as the bible says, "patience is a virtue." Be patient with your life and your path. Please don't compare your current position to anyone else's. Flowers don't all grow at the same speed and that is the same with you. Comparing yourself to another flower will not make you grow or bloom any faster. So, be still and know that God is your peace and he will bring you joy even in sorrowful and dry seasons. Mr. Theodore Roosevelt once said, 'Comparison is the thief of joy", and that my friend is so true. If you are honest with yourself, you normally aren't happy when you compare yourself to someone else. But I believe for you to stop this bad habit, you must first admit your problem. If you don't think you have a problem then you won't try to do better, because you don't see the problem, or will not face and admit the problem.

In life, we can be so adamant on fixing others and finding other's problems that we overlook our own. After admitting your problem, you should then talk to someone. For me, I talked to my sister Akeima and she was extremely non – judgmental, loving, and caring. She simply just wanted the best for me. You too should talk to someone that you know loves and cares about your well-being.

Someone you feel comfortable talking to, someone that wants to see you well and not someone who isn't a good influence. I used to think I could handle everything on my own and that I could bottle up all my emotions and that would be easier than expressing how I truly felt. But when I talked to my sister Akeima, I started to feel free and that heavy burdened was lifted. I really believed that everything was going to be okay and I could get through anything. Talking to her helped us begin to truly develop a real relationship. I really believe that burdens of shame, guilt, and sadness are real things that can only be taken off in response to a real experience or person. Communicating and releasing what is happening within is so vital to you really becoming the best version of yourself. So, right now if you feel a weight in your heart that feels unbearable, please find someone and express yourself. But let's say you truly feel like you can't talk to any human. You can ALWAYS talk to God, God loves us. People don't just send their only begotten son to die for anybody. And when you start talking to God you too, like Akeima and I, will have a true friendship. God is the true fulfiller, if you ever feel numb or empty. Go to God, I promise you, he is real. I know he is. I remember a few months ago, I felt empty and that something was missing. At that time, I hadn't been praying or reading my bible. I felt mentally and physically sick. I remember going to youth service. I went to the altar and I cried out and casted all my burdens on God. Almost instantly, that void I felt was fulfilled. God is a void filler. That story might mean nothing to you, but while writing this tears come to my eyes because I remember the internal pain and agony I felt, and no one could do anything but God himself and he did. There is this song entitled, "Refiner" by Maverick City and it simply says in the chorus, "You're a fire, the **refiner**, I wanna be consumed." Those words ring so loud in my heart because if you know what a refiner is you'll understand the power of our God. A refiner is pretty much a person, device, or substance that removes impurities, or other unwanted matters from something. So, what the song is saying is that God is the one who removes the things within us that is not giving him glory and that are not bringing us closer to the person who he has called us to be. In my opinion, we can only find true wholeness in God and God alone. The great, Maya Angelou said it best, "You don't need another person, place or thing to make you whole. God already did that. Your job is just to know it."

All in all though, I realized that it will happen. I will at times compare myself, but that shouldn't make me stop loving myself and make me believe I am any less than anyone else. I've realized that comparing yourself and validation works hand in hand. Like when you post that picture on Instagram and you only get 89 likes, so you delete it because you felt that you should've gotten 100, that is you seeking validation. But, that's the wrong validation. In that instance you are hungering people's approval but the right kind is when you are being given appreciation or approval but please know you don't need approval to be who you are. Remember that a truly strong person does not need the approval of others just like a lion doesn't need the approval from a sheep for anything. When you stop seeking approval people you will become the most free and liberated version of yourself and that is when you will be at your best. At some point in all of our lives we have been validated, whether it be by our parents, teachers, or friends and it's natural but it becomes an issue when we are constantly seeking that validation and can only make decisions with that validation. According to Webster Merriam the word validation means, "an act, process, or instance of validating; especially: the determination of the degree of validity of a measuring device." I am proud to say that I don't seek validation from anyone anymore but GOD! He should be the only person you should seek validation from. I believe that sometimes we as humans fall into the trap of seeking validation without even knowing it. It is important to understand that all of us are valid, with or without another's approval. None of us become are *invalid* without it. Please understand that people's judgment has always and only holds the value we give it. I really believe that no one can deeply hurt you or tell you something you don't already feel about yourself. In other words, if I am insecure about my smile and someone says something about it I am going to be really hurt. Now, it is definitely wrong for that person to speak on my smile but in this situation it becomes less about them and more about me and my festering insecurity. I really believe that we as humans have a lot of festering insecurities that we haven't dealt with but they make an appearance every once in a while. But, until we deal with them heads on, they will always be an issue and keep popping up like those pin thingies at the arcade that you hit with a mallet.

However, I must say that sometimes people say things that are hurtful but you may not be necessarily insecure about whatever they said, it could've simply just been a really mean statement. I can remember once I was told that I looked like Barney which sounds so simple and childish and yes I know that I don't look like Barney but it still really hurt my feelings and I even googled Barney to make sure that I didn't look like him and I remember crying at the thought that I even allowed that person and mean statement to have that much control over me. It is so important for you to know who you are and to not doubt yourself but to be confident in who God says that you are. Lao Tzu once said "Because one believes in oneself, one doesn't try to convince others. Because one is content with oneself, one doesn't need others approval. Because one accepts oneself, the world accepts him or her". When you are TRULY confident within yourself you won't feel like the victim, you won't feel less than, you will feel just right, just like when Goldilocks found the right porridge at the bears house. Her journey was bumpy but she found the porridge that was just right for her and you too will feel just right with who you are and how you were created. When you stop comparing yourself you will not seek people's approval because well, you won't need it because you have yours and God's.

When you realize how beautiful and amazing you are no matter what anyone tells you, you won't seek validation anymore, I promise.

I remember I went to church one Sunday when I was in my early teens and I wore what I thought was a beautiful dress and no one complimented me. This is a perfect example of the seeking of validation. Anyway, I told my friend Zimmie that no one complimented me and that I was sad, and she asked, "Did you like the dress?" I responded yes. She then said, "that's all that matters, your opinion is all that matters." In that moment, I really didn't care what anyone thought about my dress I just cared about how I felt. But don't get me wrong, if your mom tells you that dress isn't flattering, you should definitely listen. It doesn't mean she's trying to hurt you, but she's trying make sure you look nice. So, what if someone doesn't compliment your hair, that doesn't make your hair any less beautiful. People's inability to see your beauty is honestly none of your business. Just stand tall in knowing who you are and pay more attention to where you are going rather than the person next to you. An unknown person once said, "Don't compare your life to others. There's no comparison between the sun and the moon. They shine when it's their time." There is room for all of us to win and succeed. Jeannie Mai once said, "you don't have to unscrew someone else's light bulb to shine." We can and will all shine when it is our time. Think of positivity as our battery life. Negativity and comparing yourself won't make you shine. If we compare ourselves, we will never truly be happy with who we are because we will be constantly spending time wishing we were someone else. I remember when I really used to compare myself with other people. I wasn't happy, I just felt so little and never enough. And if I'm being honest, I still sometimes compare myself. But each day I'm trying to do better at everything I say, act, and do.

The key is to make sure it doesn't affect how it makes you feel about yourself. But when you truly begin to love you and know that you are the only you, you won't compare you will congratulate. For example, if you see your friend do something awesome congratulate, don't compare. Because your time to shine will come and it possibly already has come but you're too busy comparing and hating that you cannot see that. Don't hate, congratulate. Don't get to the place where comparing yourself is a lifestyle, and when you see something you think instantly think, "Why I couldn't have that right away? That is not healthy. Your reaction should be of celebration for that person not hatred. When your friend wins, that doesn't mean you lose. I understand there are people in the world like Beyoncé and Oprah and Michelle Obama, how could you not compare yourself to them? They have money, fame, and influence but you too have those things in your own way. We all have some influence, we all know somebody that knows you and you clearly have at least $20 because you have this book in your hand. But seriously use what you have, if all you have are lemons make some lemonade. If all you have are apples make apple juice, use what you have. Start where you are and use what you can. And remember, you don't know the process that Oprah, Beyonce, and Michelle Obama went through to become who they are.

They didn't just wake up and become the living legends they are, but they worked for it and you must work for it too. Yes, Beyoncé is absolutely beautiful and beyond talented, but she is not you and you will never be her and that is okay. You can try to imitate her, but what good does that do for you? You can emulate her skills, attitudes, and characteristic but not them as a person. We don't need 100 wanna be Beyoncé's in the world. When we can have other amazing, talented, and unique artists. If we all strived to be like one person other than Jesus himself, this thing called life would be absolutely horrible. Be who you are and know that you are more than enough and yes, everything takes a process. But, make the declaration now, that I am the only me and that is my power. Don't compare yourself with anyone in this world. What we don't realize is that when we insult ourselves we are also insulting our creator (which is God) and you don't want to insult God or yourself. And the thing is, is that we are all at different stages and phases in our lives. So, she might be on her A-game today and you are on your C game. You guys are at two completely different stages so it's not fair to compare. Would it be fair to make a 50-year-old mathematician go against an 8-year-old boy who is learning 1+1, no it wouldn't because there at different stages in life. The reason we at times struggle with our insecurities is because we compare our rehearsals with someone else's performance. You can't do that, that's not fair to yourself. How are you going to enjoy your life if you are constantly comparing it to others? Don't compare your weaknesses to someone else's strengths, again that's just not fair. It's like comparing an apple and a box of fried chicken, like obviously the apple is healthier, but the chicken taste really good. So, we all have good qualities and the person your comparing has good qualities, so at the end of the day, it's a win-win. Regardless if they're rich and your poor or you're happy and they're sad, you both are amazing. Comparing two amazing things is extremely hard and unfair to both. The point is comparing yourself is pointless as well as unhealthy. When you compare yourself, there is no goal accomplished but tearing yourself down. Everything you say and do should have a positive objective.

Growing up having two sisters like 10 years older than me, I always tried

to emulate them, and they were in the stage in their life where they would be getting their life together. So, I thought when I was around 8 years old that I needed to get my life together too. So, I beat myself up for not being like them. But, what I failed to realize is that we were all at 3 completely distinctly different levels in our lives. Another thing is, we don't think about the people we compare ourselves too. What do you mean by that Robyn? I mean that we only compare the good stuff about people. You've never heard someone say I wish I had sadness and not anger, never! For example, Demi Lovato, she is such a talented, beautiful and awesome woman and she's rich. Now you might think yea I wish I was her! Her life is awesome, but do you know what she's been through. She has a bipolar disorder and she's going through an eating disorder. Now I'm not saying those things to say that now she's all of a sudden, a bad person. She can't control any of those things. But if anything, that makes her even more of an awesome and amazing person that she is getting through it. But, don't want to be people, want to have attributes like them or to be as driven. You can be inspired without wanting to be that person. But be happy with who you are, because if you were given some of the problems that the people you compare yourself to had to face, you probably would be pretty happy with who you are, or you just could not handle it.

Dennis Prager once said, "If you don't factor in everything about whoever you are comparing yourself to you're playing a mix and match game that doesn't exist in the real world". We have to be honest with ourselves if we want to be successful and stop doing something we do on a regular basis like comparing ourselves. Be your own measure of success. That means that you don't base how good you're doing by other people's success, but rather by how bad you were doing yesterday. For example, if I have a problem with lying, I'm not going to say, "that girl Lindsay is so honest, why can't I be like Lindsay." I'm going to say Robyn you lied eight times yesterday and today you only lied 4 times, you're getting better. Measure your success on your own performance. Another thing, be happy with who and where you are, enjoy the process of life. You don't always have to be on 10. No one is always on 10. If you're sad cry, don't make anyone make you feel an emotion you don't have. I'm not saying be at the same level for all your life. But, if your sad, be sad, don't dwell on it forever. But don't make someone force you to be sad or happy if you don't feel those emotions. I hate when people say, 'cheer up" when I am crying, like let me cry. I feel that crying is very healthy, crying is a language that no one understands but God. Crying is a release that is unexplainable. Truly feel every emotion you have and never make people make you feel an emotion you are not feeling. I truly believe in my heart that the best and most beautiful things in the world cannot be seen or touched and I believe that our emotions are one of those things.

Life is like a journey and we are all on different parts of the trail, it's a process, be okay with the process. All I'm saying is don't be so hard on yourself and just don't compare, you will literally go nowhere in life if all you do is compare. For example, imagine you were on Forbes Top 10 List of Richest People in the World and you were #9. Comparison and insecurity will make you upset and envy the 8 people who are richer than you. Do you understand how dumb that sounds?, and it's okay to be ambitious but there are levels to it. But if you keep comparing, that is what it will do to you, you will constantly be discontent and no one wants to live unhappy and never satisfied. Chaka Khan said something so powerful once, she said, "America breeds ambition and while that can be a good thing, sometimes it's not. Ambition also breeds competition and that can be a very bad thing. People become chronically preoccupied with competing and don't know when to stop. It can become unhealthy." Life is all about balance. Be ambitious but also be grateful for where you are in the process because if not you will drive yourself downhill. We as humans have to learn about balance and the importance of resting and contentment. I once heard J. Cole say in an interview that if your aim is to have lots of money, you will never be satisfied because there will always be more and more money to have. Just know that where you are and who you are is okay. Grow and also know that life is about seasons and allowing yourself to progress and naturally transition into the person you were created to be. Yes, have ambition and yes have wisdom, they both work hand in hand.

You are beautiful and amazing, and you are literally the only you. Why compare that to Beyoncé or Bill Gates or Oprah, you must be so confident that you won't want to take or be in their seat at the table but you will want to join the seat at their table or build your own table that they can join one day. Always remember, aim to admire someone else's beauty without questioning your own. Comparison is extremely unhealthy but can be so natural and we can do it without even trying. But, truly know that you are amazing, and you are the only you and that's never worth comparing.

chapter 4.

Influential Voices:

Family, Friends and the people around you

Invest in people who invest in you. Growing up, I was always the youngest in the group, everyone was older. So, I wasn't sure who my friends were. I wasn't sure that spending time with them, made them my friends. I have a friend named Zeandra (Zimmie) she and I are 5 years apart. She is such a genuinely beautiful and kind hearted person. Well other than sometimes not answering the phone lol. But, she is a really pleasant and loving individual. I struggled with not understanding our relationship. We talked all the time, but I wasn't sure if we were friends because of our age difference. So being the honest and upfront person I am, I talked to her about it. She said assuringly, "girl we're sisters," and in that moment, I knew she cared. I honestly didn't care what we were, I cared that I had someone who influenced me in a positive way and loved me for me.

This chapter might be my favorite because I'm talking about the people that I love. I have key people in my life that I can pretty much talk to about anything. You too should have those people because they help to develop the best you. The people around you are honestly a reflection of who you are. A few of those people are my sisters Martina and Akeima. I have my Aunty Jay, I have Kaylee, I have Jaaquan (my one true guy's perspective on everything), I have Kayla, I have Enzoe, I have Xaria, I have Jaelyn, I have Tia, I have my Mommy and I have the Lord.

But before we go on, let's talk about the guy perspective thing. Jaaquan is my guy perspective/influential voice. I think it is vital to have a male perspective in everything because, well girls are usually emotional, and guys aren't as emotional, especially not Jaaquan, so he will not give you an emotional answer but a harsh but honest answer. Guys will give the guy perspective on things and not the girly one. Females and males look at life from very different perspectives and that's natural because we're two different genders. So, thank you Jaaquan (lol). So those are my influential voices. I have others who influence me but these are the main ones. Having those key people who guide you in the right direction is extremely important in becoming the best you possible.

Friendship is so important; having someone you can talk to about anything, someone who doesn't judge you, but helps you and someone you know is always there. Having friends are vital to the human experience, they love you, cry with you and they pray with you.

My best friend Kayla is the perfect example of this, although she sometimes takes her time to call me back (shade but no shade) I know without a doubt she is always there for me through anything. Kayla and I are very different but I have realized

Influential Voices 75

in our relationship that those differences make us perfectly work. She is so quiet yet loud. She is so sweet yet mean but it all works out because I am the same way. Kayla has taught me so much and the main thing that I have learned is that not everyone will show their love the same but that doesn't mean they don't love you. Kayla has never been super expressive and extra with showing her love for me but it's in the simple things that has shown me her love. I remember we hadn't seen each other in a while and she dropped by my house out of the blue and brought me macaroni and I was forever grateful for that because it was an expression of her love. Another memory we have that makes me so happy is the time that we went to the store and bought my homecoming dress the day before homecoming which was crazy and so emotional and tiring. I've realized that just because someone may not show their love how you're used to, it doesn't mean they're not showing you love.

You know, people really don't have those key people in their life, so if you do, you are truly blessed and should be grateful. Friendship is so vital in the process of realizing that "You Are the Only You' because they remind you of that and they keep you accountable. You should surround yourself with the dreamers and the doers, the believers and the thinkers. But, most of all always surround yourself with those who see greatness within you, even when you don't see it in yourself. The amazing and illustrious Oprah Winfrey once said," Surround yourself with only people who are going to lift you higher. "Your family and friends are so important because you're always around them, so they play a fundamental role in your development. We're all like babies. We're a product of our environment. If your mom, dad, sisters, and brothers curse that's probably what you are going to do. Not always but it's more than likely bound to happen. That is why you have to be careful with who and what you let in your space. Now, I know you can't always control who and what comes around you but when you can, be intentional about that and when you can't, you have to find a way to protect your peace. And when it comes to family, I know you necessarily can't tell your parents to stop cursing or shouting , but you can write a letter, express how it makes you feel or if push comes to shove just try to block it out. However though, please know that you don't have to follow their example, you can change your own path. You don't have to be what you saw. Sometimes because of the people around us we feel that we have to conform, but we don't. Don't be easily influenced, it's easier said than done but it can be done. When you have to start compromising yourself and your morals because of the people around you, you need to change the people you are around.

Influential Voices are people who pour into you, who say things that can affect you. Now, it important to know that you can have bad influential voices. But then that's when you must choose either to become their good influential voice or you distance yourself from them. I do not believe in cutting people off or cancelling people. I believe in distancing myself but first communicating the problem so they know why the distancing is happening. In my experience, nowadays people are so easy to just drop people and I don't think that's right. Especially if you have history with that person and no I am not saying stay friends because you have history but really do the kind and respectful thing. I always try to leave every relationship in love, maybe not always good terms, but in love. Sometimes, some situations you can't communicate to the person, but try to distance not cut off, especially if you say that this person is important to you. Try to leave every relationship on good terms, key word try.

The reality is, many people come from many different backgrounds of families and sometimes those families aren't nice to them so because of that they treat the people around them with that same attitude. People do what they are taught and the only way they do anything different is if they intentionally unlearn somethings. When you have a friend, they are more than likely treating you the way they have been taught and molded into treating people. Patience is so important when being someone's friend because ultimately we are all learning and growing. Show the same grace, love, and understanding you want to be shown. The definition of friend according to the Webster Merriam, "is one attached to another by affection or esteem."

When I was younger, I had a best friend and we were extremely close. We were always at each other's house, we played games, went to church together, and ate a lot of food. Regular best friends stuff; but then we grew apart. She was in 8th grade and I was in 5th grade it wasn't weird, but I realized things were changing. I personally to this day, don't really like change. I like having the same friends and the same habits. I don't like being uncomfortable or unprepared, which isn't healthy but it's something I'm working on. So, when I realized our relationship was changing, I became kind of annoyed and sad at the same time. But there was something different about this change. Our changed friendship changed I how I dealt with change. I know that was a lot of change for one sentence. But it honestly shaped every other change in my life that came after. I did something I had never done before. I didn't fight it, I didn't beg for the relationship, I just let go and let God do what he wanted. It actually affected me in a positive way. It didn't feel positive in the moment, but now that I've gone through it, I know it was for the best. Now when I feel things are about to change I pray, express how I feel, and continue living. I don't let it affect how I feel about myself because ultimately change is inevitable and change comes with the territory of friendship. There is this song entitled, "Let Go" by Paul Morton and my favorite part says, "As soon as I stop worrying, worrying how the story ends, when I let go and I let God, let God have his way. That's when things start happening when I stopped looking at bad things, when I let go and I let God, let God have his way." This song is speaking absolute facts, when we let go and just let God do what he wants in our lives and our relationships that is when we true change begins to happen. One thing that I must say, is that you have to let go of your unexpressed expectations. Let me explain, I feel that we as humans have many expectations going into relationships and that's okay and very natural. But, the issue comes in when those expectations are not expressed and then we are mad at our friends for something they didn't even know they needed to do. So, you either need to express your desires or let them go because honestly, most times we don't express them because we ourselves aren't willing to do what we want them to do. And yes, have standards and hold people accountable but don't demand something you are unwilling to give. There are some relationships you are going to have to fight for and some you have to let go. But it is all depending on the relationship and the person, you will have to decide if it's worth the fight. It truly just depends, but in this case, I just had to let go of the friendship that we once had.

The most important thing in any relationship is communication. Communication truly will make or break your relationships. Overall, in my situation there would always be an age gap. So, we would have to decide if that would be something worth figuring out or just letting go. I was going to middle school and she was going to high school. When I went to high school, she would be going to college. The gap would only widen with time. Like I said I didn't truly know who my true friends were at that time in my life because they were like always 10 years older than me. When friendships end or transition to a different level it always isn't a bad thing. It can actually help you become a better person. Sometimes you both are great people, but just not great together and there's nothing wrong with that. My friend Jaaquan once told me, "Imagine that you are a test and your friend is an answer sheet. But their answers aren't the correct answers for your test. That's okay, they're an answer sheet, just not the right one for you. We are both still really close friends and love each other very much. But there are stages to friendships and we are not where we were. Again which is okay. Understand that people change and sometimes they are no longer compatible with you and that's just life. It may hurt, but in the long haul, you will learn so much and will be grateful for every change that took place. Influential voices will not always be there. I believe that some influential voices are for different seasons, some are not meant forever. Once you learn to accept leaving some relationships behind, it becomes easier and will honestly help you in blooming into the person you were destined to be.

Influential voices are people that you can comfortably voice your feelings and opinions to. You should feel free and liberated with your friends. And even when the relationship may come to an end, I pray that you still have a sense of respect for them because going out and spilling all there tea after you stop being friends is childish and immature. Not just that but friendships that break don't always have to stay broken forever. I had another best friend named Jonathan when I was like in the third grade, he was like the best friend ever. He was a really kind person and his Grandfather was a pastor, so we related in that sense too. But our friendship broke because he said a few things that really hurt me. So, we did not talk for like two years. One day about two years later, I decided to text him. I told him that I did not like how we just broke off. Now you might be thinking, that is a long time. But he said something that was extremely disrespectful. From the beginning of the friendship I set the standard and my expectation. I said that I would not tolerate something like that and he knew I was serious. There was no bye it was just over. I never told him I was upset about what he said, I just distanced myself. So, I decided to tell him how I felt. He apologized and now we are cool. We are still close, and I am super glad that I made the decision to not let that stop our friendship. My sister Martina actually was the one who told me I should tell him how I felt, so thanks sister and that's why you should still stay in character even if the friendship ends because you never know what the future may hold.

Life sometimes feels like it's going super-fast and we can feel like we are running out of time. Moreover, that's why when I can, I try to deal with friendship conflicts either when they happen or soon after they happen. I am the type of person who cannot just continue like nothing happened, after something clearly happened. I have to confront, and I have to tell the person how I feel. I feel that is healthy because if you just act like nothing happened, then you will have unsolved business in the air and yes sometimes the best communication is moments of silence but using our words are important too. A wise woman once said, " A lack of communications breeds assumptions of what the other person is thinking or feeling and assumptions are more often than not, incorrect."

Now, when I lost and drifted from my first true best friend, I tried to put more effort in having friends at school. I had lots of "friends" at school. But most of my "school friends" were honestly just people I had to kindly tolerate for 180 days of the year. So, I didn't really have a choice but to like them, I was stuck. I was extremely social, all the teachers liked me, and I was friendly. But, once I started talking and getting to really know people, I ended up with an amazing friend, Kaylee. She is the sweetest ever and super smart. She is honestly my first true friend at school that I truly love and loved talking to. She understood me and accepted me for who I was and what I stood for. I remember once when I was fasting in elementary school and some people thought that I was crazy, Kaylee never did and she supported me through it. And that is why, for me, my friends have to think, act, and be a certain way. It's not that I think I'm Miss Holier than thou, but the people around you (our influential voices) are a representation of who we are and after meeting certain influential voices, I knew that it would be possible to find people who supported me being me, because for a long time I didn't think I could find anyone, but I did and I could. So, it is important for you to stay positive and be very mindful of knowing that who you hang around in a way is a reflection of who you are. So, one thing that I really stand by is that I would prefer that my true friends don't curse around me which is super rare in our society as a whole and you may be thinking, "that's extra" but that's okay because you don't have to be my friend (lol... but seriously, everyone is different and that's what I would personally prefer and that is okay). So, that's one of my standards or expectations in a friendship. Another expectation is that you have to be a genuinely and intentionally kind person. There are so many negative spirited people in the world and those people need to be prayed for not my friends, sorry God. But, why would I want a really mean person to be my friend? Unless God himself sent them, I don't want them. You have to be very intentional with who and what you allow in your personal space. Some friends may good people but not good for you and what one person may be able to deal with you may not and that is okay too. Daniell Koepke who is such a great writer, once said that, "Not all toxic people are cruel and uncaring. Some of them love us dearly. Many of them have good intentions. Most are simply toxic to our being simply because their needs and way of existing force us to compromise ourselves and our happiness." A big part of successfully navigating through relationships and specifically friendships is compromising and figuring out what is truly important to you as a person. However though, there are some things that you should never compromise and you yourself have to decide what those things are. Now for the people struggling to make friends, I understand it can be hard and really discouraging especially if you just lost a friend, it can be hard to trust again. But, just know that you will make friends again and I was once told that the best time to make friends is before you need them. Things that I would suggest is to just say hi, be nice, be approachable, and have a welcoming attitude. When you do those things, it shows that you're putting in effort. It shows that you want to talk to them, so they'll likely respond with the same attitude. It's like that saying everyone says, "Treat people the way you want to be treated." If you start the conversation with a good attitude, then they'll respond back with that same attitude, hopefully, at least. If they don't that's fine they're not meant to be your friend anyway. But the thing about friendships is that they change you for the better or worse. That's where becoming the best you comes into play. So, if your bestie is smoking, is she a good influence and helping you to be the best you, if smoking is not something you want to engage in (not really). So, in that case, you can TRY to be her influential voice, but that just depends on how strong you are because you might try and end up smoking with her. Now in that case, still be careful because no matter how strong you are and that you think you are, you are still human so honestly you might have to let that friendship go. And don't get me wrong, you may well be able not to indulge in what your friends are doing because I have friends who do things that I honestly don't ever see or plan on doing and I have made that intentional decision. However, it would definitely be easier to not do or think about whatever activity it is if it wasn't being done around me and that's why you have to do what you know you need to do for the betterment of you. Especially, if it's something you are trying to stop doing. It's like if you have a drinking problem and then all your friends are drinking around you, that doesn't help at all. So, depending on the situation you honestly may have to distance yourself away from that relationship and you know, I almost said you may have to cut that person off. But, like I've said I personally don't believe in cutting people off, at first. I believe in communicating you don't want to be in the relationship anymore. Then distance yourself; don't just cut the cord. I also believe if you truly cared about them to begin with, you wouldn't be able to just cut them off with no remorse, but that's for another book, never mind.

All in all though, you can have a friend who uplifts you, tells you, you can do anything you put your mind to. You could have a friend who prays with you, who laughs with you, and who doesn't judge you but looks at your situation/problem and gives you wise advice. Or you can have a friend who is negative, acts nice in front of you but talks behind your back, prays for your downfall, and is mean-spirited. You ultimately decide which one you choose and you decide how your friend's actions will impact you. Not all friends start off bad but when you realize that they're changing you in a negative way because of their influence, you either can communicate the problem or break ties. You should definitely attempt to tell them how you truly feel, because you don't need anyone stopping you from reaching your highest potential, we ourselves do that enough to ourselves, you don't need your friend doing the same. Now, sometimes communication isn't enough, and you have to break ties, but you have to use your own discretion in that situation.

Now, anyway it's important that you have standards for yourself not just for your friends but for you. Say to yourself that, I will not indulge in that conversation, or I will not say those words, or I will not listen to that music or I won't let these words be spoken to me. A true influential voice/friend will help you hold yourself to that standard. Also, realize that you as a friend have major influence on your friend. They hang around you a lot and watch how you handle yourself. So be very careful that you are showing your friends a good way of living, especially if you say you're a Christian. A true friend isn't just someone you hang out with but someone who challenges you to look more like Jesus every day. There is a tool that Christians use to win souls called, Evangelism. It's when you tell people about God, but I believe even before we do that the biggest way we can evangelize is through our lifestyle. Is your life even a little bit of a reflection of Jesus Christ? Are you being a positive influential voice? Is your life leading people in the right direction and I'm not trying to get preachy or put pressure on you but if you are a Christian, then these are the conversations you need to be having, your actions matter. And I'm not saying live for people or live right because others are watching but having a sense of awareness of that is so important. The truth is, is that all influential voices aren't positive and all aren't negative, so you have to be able to discern who is who. It's crazy the amount of influence that we have on people even just as regular people, who aren't celebrities. You don't have to be rich and famous to influence people, you honestly just have to be a human. But you can't influence the world if you act just like it. I have power. I am powerful. I will and can change the world. Say these things to yourself and that will not only help you but it will encourage you to become the best you possible. The more you influence yourself, the more you will be able to influence others. I believe you must be influential to yourself before you can truly influence others. I've created 3 main ways that I feel that you can influence yourself in a positive manner. So, here they are.

1. **Invest in yourself;** if you want to be a fashion designer, buy a sewing machine or sign up for sewing classes. If you want to be an actress take acting classes, train yourself to memorize lines. If you want to be a doctor, start learning terms that all doctors need to know. If you have a dream prepare yourself and start getting yourself together to accomplish that dream. Dreams will stay dreams if you don't wake up and do something about it. Publishing this book took so long and it was all seriously because I was being lazy and kept dreaming of pub-

lishing it but I wasn't taking the necessary steps to accomplish it. It is not enough to say that you want something, you have to go after it. Do something today that will make your future self say thank you. Then repeat that every day. Consistency is key. Maybe its reading this book, maybe it's going jogging, and maybe it's to start to take more risk, just do it because you're going to thank yourself for doing it now. Close your eyes and jump! Following your passions can sometimes be scary and intimidating but if it was easy, everyone would be doing it. Put time and energy into you and your passions. You know, at times we're so worried about other people and their goals and their aspirations and we forget about our own. Don't forget about yourself. Don't invest more in others than yourself. Yes, help people, but don't set yourself on fire to take out someone else's fire out. Never underestimate the investment you make in yourself. I truly believe that one of the best investments you can ever make is one in yourself, remember that.

2. **Encourage Yourself**. Look at yourself into the mirror every day and tell yourself you can do this and you will do this. You will be kind and you will be the best version of yourself today. Lift your own self up. Don't wait on someone to accomplish your goals and tell yourself you're amazing. Although that is what influential voices do, you cannot become so dependent on them that you can't push your own self because the reality is, sometimes they won't be there and that's okay. You have

to always be there for you. You have to be your own biggest cheerleader. You have to know that you are the bomb.com. Chile, you are already a sundae, people's compliments are just the whip cream, sprinkles, and cherry on top. (and remember the sundae is already good by itself). This section reminds me of this song that I love to sing throughout my days, its entitled *Encourage Yourself* and my favorite line says, "sometimes you have to speak victory during the test." I love that because we face test and trials all the time but even through that, you really should speak victory and claim that it won't last forever. I say should instead of must because I understand that sometimes it feels like it's over and you feel hopeless. But, you must keep fighting and keep encouraging yourself. And sometimes the people around you aren't being supportive and even your influential voices think you should give up. But, you have to be the one to be there for you and encourage yourself, no matter how you feel. Encourage yourself. Joel Osteen once said, "When nobody celebrates you, celebrate yourself. When nobody else compliments you, compliment yourself. It's not up to other people to keep you encouraged but it's up to you. "Encouragement should come from the inside. Now don't get me wrong those influential voices are vital and very important, but your biggest fan should be you. If you don't believe in you, who will? One day I saw my mom painting her toes for this wedding we were attending and she was wearing closed toed shoes and I said, "Mommy no one is going to see your toes." Then, she said, "When you care, people care, you don't do things for others, but you do them for yourself and then they won't take you for granted." I then responded, "That is such a good quote mommy, I can put in my book" (lol). Side note: I find it so funny that my mom turned the simplest thing into a whole TedTalk. Anyway though, seriously buy those $100 shoes, not because someone will like them but because you like them. Show love to yourself for you. Splurge on yourself, once in a while for you. Be the only you for you.

3. **Make a Plan**. Write down your goals for your day, week, month, year, or your life and find feasible and workable ways to actually accomplish them. Don't think about the what ifs but think about the how's. We cheat ourselves out of amazing ideas and opportunities by questioning ourselves. If I'm honest, I was extremely afraid to write this book. I thought, "No one is going to care about what this 12 year old girl (that was the age I was when I started writing) has to say." But hopefully I can say that this was a New York Times Best Seller or honestly if it just impacted one life, but if I kept questioning myself it would have never happened. Every day I write down or type 'My Day My Life' that is pretty much a title for the list of all the things I want to accomplish for that day and it helps me get things done and be organized. I'll show you an example:

Doing this, helps me be the best me and it keeps me very efficient, which we should all aim to be. I once read something that said, and I quote, "Nobody ever wrote down a plan to be broke, lazy or stupid. Those things are what happen when you don't have a plan". Which is entirely true, when you don't have a plan you are just wishing and a goal without a plan is a wish. An incredible man once said, "If you don't design your own life plan, chances are you'll fall into someone else plan. And guess what they have planned for you? Not much." You are the driver of your own life and yes God ultimately is but we can't just sit and ask God to do stuff for us like he is a Jeannie. We have to do what needs to be done to get what we desire. Remember it all just starts with a plan, even if it's a small plan just have a plan, although, you should go big or go home. But at least try. You never know unless you try. It is better to try and fail then fail to try.

I believe if you do these 3 things you will be influencing people in the process of doing them without even knowing. An influential voice is what you want to be, nobody wants to be a boring person that people look down upon. And, remember don't be afraid of yourself for being an influential voice. Sometimes we're afraid of telling our friends and family the truth and then they end up looking bad in the end. My mom always said, "I'd rather tell you than have someone outside tell you." Be that influential voice that nurtures, but also tells the truth. But remember even though you are influencing others it doesn't mean you won't be influenced. So be careful who you are influenced by and don't get a big head. By that I mean, don't think you're too good to be influenced because that's a long dark path you don't want to walk through. Make sure your being influenced by something or someone who is uplifting you and not tearing you down. Remember influence means the power to have an important effect on someone or something. This shows that you are important and what you say and do can influence people in the right or wrong direction. So be very mindful. If someone influences someone else, they are changing a person in an indirect but very important way. You are probably already that influential voice and you don't know it.(no pressure) Someone is watching your every move, not in a creepy way, but they are. Whether you believe it or not, you give someone hope. John Shelby Spong once said, "If you begin to give people hope that there is a brighter future, there is a new tomorrow, then the people who were yesterday's terrorists become tomorrow's elected officials and they're part of the change of the system."

Influential voices are the people around you that tell you the truth. They love you and make sure you're okay. Influential voices are all around you. But I believe that God has assigned specific ones for specific people and you get to choose them too. Influential voices are designated by God for you, to help you accomplish and succeed in this thing called life confidently and successfully. A true friend is equivalent to an influential voice. As I said at the beginning of this chapter, I was not sure who my friends were because of my age difference. But, what I have realized is that truly age is nothing but a number.(not like R.Kelly but you know what I mean) You can have a 40-year-old influential voice and you can have a 12-year-old influential voice. Influential voices are the people who help you become the best you and any age can help you do that. So, be careful how you treat those young or old people because they could be your future influential voice, or they can be your influential voice now and you don't even know it because you are judging them from a surface level.

Influential voices are people that live life to the fullest and are supportive of the people around them. They truly demonstrate what being the only you truly means and they help you know that you too are the only you. I want to influence people. I want someone to look at me and say because of you I didn't give up, and that my friend is a true influential voice.

chapter 5

Know Your Worth

Do not take any and anything from anybody. We as individuals are all so beautiful and unique, and we should never just allow people to walk all over us and be to mean us. Growing up I was always the youngest wherever I went. I believe that because of me being younger I didn't truly understand my worth. I at times didn't really understand that even though I was young that I still had a voice and that what I felt mattered. I have in the past allowed people to be mean to me and honestly just make me feel less than because of my age. I allowed people to say whatever to me simply because I was younger than them and for many that may be normal or something that is accepted. But,

I feel that belittling a person and especially a young person's voice can ultimately tear down that young person's self-esteem. I would allow the older kids around me ultimately make me feel inferior and like I had no sense of my own. I remember when I was way younger, I went to a service on a Friday night during my church's annual youth conference. I was super excited to do a particular style to my hair for the service and I asked my god mom "Aunty Jay" to do it for me. In my opinion, I thought it was super cute and that I was going to look great. I bought a new dress and everything, I was ready to style and profile. But, this girl and her sister had other thoughts. They told me my hairstyle made me look like a dinosaur. Now, besides the tremendous hurt it brought me, it was also a very ironic situation because I actually saw them do the style multiple times and I was just trying to copy them and honestly just look like the big girls. When they said it, I was completely devastated, and I cried. At this time, I'm around eight years old and I never stood up for myself. Because of my age I just felt voiceless around certain people and would rather to just be quiet instead of expressing how I was feeling when in the end I knew I probably would just get shut down. I must say though, that feeling of feeling voiceless and belittled didn't come from my family but came from certain older kids that I would hang around. Now, other similar small situations would happen, and I sometimes would say something, but I normally didn't. I felt that it was honestly pointless. As I got older, I would respond but not intelligently, so it didn't really make a difference. But as I got older, I realized that if I truly loved myself, I would advocate for myself. In doing this I would ensure that I was treated with the same respect that any person should be treated with. And I understand that when you are younger, it is natural to feel small and treated small in many ways because you are small but in my opinion you should always be treated with love and respect. I believe that every human being deserves respect and love, regardless of the age. Respect is something that a lot of people love speaking about but are very stingy on giving out. Respect should be given to the old, young and middle in age. Now, I do believe that there is a difference between respect and honor. **Respect** by definition is having due regard for the feelings, wishes, rights, or traditions of others and *Honor* is defined as high respect and esteem of someone. So, I am not saying that the youth deserve to be shown honor but they should be spoken to and treated with respect and so does everyone other human on this planet. In knowing your worth, respect is a vital piece in this puzzle because if you cannot respect everyone around you then you can't truly respect yourself and vice versa. If you cannot respect yourself then you can't truly respect others. Respect should be given to the garbage man and to the doctor. Respect should be given to the teacher and to the astronaut. Respect should be given to all, even the disrespectful which sounds wrong but its right. If someone is disrespectful, you don't have to rub love and respect all in their face but you can acknowledge their presence and show them how you should be treated. In a weird way, I feel that we show people how to treat us by how we treat them. Like I said in a past chapter, you cannot demand something you are not willing to give.

So anyhow, after I learned so much through the experiences I faced in regard of feeling small. I had a true epiphany. Due to all of those moments, I now know how much I am worth and having that knowledge and assurance within yourself is priceless. I am God's child, so no one can treat me however they want. I now know how much I am worth. I am priceless, I am a rare jewel, I am beautiful, and no one gets to treat me anyway they would like to.

So, I tell you, defend yourself, don't allow people to speak to you any kind of way.

You are queen and kings, people don't treat kings and queens any and anyhow. When you know your worth, you won't take any and anything from people. Don't allow people to be mean to you, stand up for yourself. Don't let people mistake your kindness for weakness or your calmness for acceptance. You set the standard of how people treat you. You deserve respect, you deserve to be treated kindly. And even writing this now, I can hear people saying that "well you aren't owed anything." I get that but having self-respect and having a healthy regard for yourself is important and I stand by the statement that you are deserving of love and respect. So yes, respect yourself and even if people in the long haul don't respect you, it's okay because you know who you are and you, respect you and that is all that matters.

Now, as your fellow human being I know that when you feel disrespected, you are going to want to respond. And I'll be dumb to believe that if I tell you to not respond, you'll actually listen. So, I advise you, if you are going to respond or clap back like some say. Clap Back intelligently. Don't respond vulgarly or even in a mean-spirited way. Respond in a way that the person you are talking to can apologize after, not in a way where another argument can be formed. Because that's the problem, many people enjoy arguing and they usually come into the disagreement with their guns blazing fire because there not looking for a solution, they just want to wallow in the frustration. So, be mindful and move accordingly of who you are dealing with in disagreements especially if it's about respect or how worthy or not worthy you are of something.

Human reading this, know your worth regardless of where you are. If you are at school or work or at the grocery store, walk with the knowing that you are all that and a bag of chips. Don't dumb down so others can look smarter, don't be snobby but don't just let people walk over you either. Don't steal the spotlight but don't push the spotlight away if it happens to come on you. Don't be humble to a fault, and that is where you just don't accept appreciation because of a complex and festering insecurity within. Don't make yourself available to people who only engage with you at their convenience. I don't care how busy someone says they are, if you are important to them they will always make you as a priority. But because you don't know your worth you will just take what you can get. That's why it's so important for you to know who you are, what you are, and whose you are. If you know your worth, if people mistreat you, although it's rude, you won't allow it to fester and hugely impact you because you know who you are.

 When on your journey to knowing you worth, you will have to learn what things you will and will not accept. At school, people curse a lot and when I say a lot I mean a lot. But I personally don't. And it's not because I'm miss goody too shoes but because it's not ladylike or manly like in my opinion. When I was as young as being in the 5th grade and in middle school, I just never stood for cursing and people would just know not to curse around me. People ultimately knew if they wanted to talk to me, I would just rather them not curse. In the 3rd and 4th grade, I had a friend and he cursed A LOT. But, when he was around me he wouldn't and couldn't or I would hit him on his arm and I wouldn't talk to him. (sorry mom and dad, I know violence is never the answer). But, it worked out because he didn't curse at all around me and when he did, he would apologize, which I thought was the cutest thing ever and I low key later on had a huge crush on him but that is another story for another time.

So, the point is that, when you set a standard and know that like my friend Jaaquan once said, "My ears aren't garbage bins and I don't want to hear your trash," you will set a standard and ultimately say, "I will not tolerate this."

When you set a standard from the beginning of any relationship, the other person will know that you will not tolerate this because from the beginning you said it and meant it. When you know your worth, you will not allow yourself to be treated or talked to any kind of way and your energy and spirit will honestly reject it. You must see yourself as important and important people aren't treated any and anyway. I believe that everyone is important because important means to have significance and I believe that we all are significant. I have an example, have you ever seen the cool kids at school being bullied?, My answer is No. They aren't bullied because they are seen as cool and although it's not the reality right now I feel like everyone should be treated with that same love and respect because we are all cool in our own ways.

I want you to know that you don't have to accept the things you are not okay with. You don't have to tolerate it. I once said in my blog that you shouldn't be in an atmosphere that you're tolerated, but where you're appreciated. Don't go into environments that you're not treated the way you deserve to be treated. They do not deserve to be in your presence if they are going to treat you in a disrespectful manner.

Growing up because I was the youngest I was not always treated nicely. I would push my way everywhere. But then over time I began to stop. I did not like going places where I was not treated properly or felt unwelcomed. You shouldn't feel uncomfortable when you are around the people you love. You should feel confident and proud of who you are everywhere you go. Don't let anyone ever break you or hurt you and let them get away with. You must stand on your own two feet and stand up for yourself. There are those that would give anything up to see you fail, but you must never give anyone that satisfaction. Hold your head up high, smile, and stand on your ground. Don't ever be bullied into silence. Stand up for what you believe in and believe in yourself. Because you believe in yourself you should stand up for yourself because you are so valuable in God's eyes and in man's eyes. But God's eyes are way more important. Choose to be kind because it makes you happy, but always without fail defend your boundaries and your loved ones without hesitation. Don't ever just walk away when someone does something to you that makes you uncomfortable.

In the 6th grade, I was touched inappropriately at school. I told my dean and nothing was done because I wasn't positive of who touched me. I didn't see his face, he just ran away. I honestly thought that I was weak for not hitting him back or running after him. I felt in a way that it was my fault, I thought maybe I shouldn't have worn that skirt or why didn't I hit him. But all of those thoughts were nonsense looking back. What you wear or don't wear is not an invitation to be touched inappropriately. This stigma of if you wear something fitted or short means that you are asking for it, is wrong because the reality is these things were happening centuries ago and all the women wore long dresses. I really believed that I didn't do all that I could. But, the thing is, what I failed to realize is that just the fact that I told someone showed that I knew my worth. I know so many girls who would be flattered if a boy touched them inappropriately which sounds weird but it's the reality because some people feel it's cute or funny. They think well he must like me, no he touched you inappropriately and you felt wrong after but didn't say anything. Don't mistake someone "liking you "and someone "assaulting you." You might think, Robyn you're being dramatic, well I'm not. People are assaulted every day and do not even know it. If they are, they're choosing to ignore it because they're afraid of what people may say or what they may think of the person. Assault in the simplest sense is physical attack. I walk around my school campus and see it all the time. The girls or boys laugh, but deep down they know it's wrong. When someone touches you without your permission, it is not that "oh he likes me" or a compliment. But rather, he feels that he can do whatever he wants and wants to look cool. But no, that's not okay and it will never and should never be okay. Know your worth and never allow someone to violate you. Sexual assault and harassment is a huge issue in our world and it's worse in some places. I want whoever is reading this, whether you are a girl or boy to know that it wasn't your fault. You should feel no shame because it wasn't your fault. It hurts my heart knowing that the people who are treated badly feel worst and are looked upon worse than the actual person who did it. It's like you making fun of a person whose house who got broken into and not the thief. Sexual harassment is just one layer of the issue but if you another layer it then reveals another really heartbreaking issue and that's rape and molestation. I get it, these are uncomfortable words and topics but it's real and more people have gone through it then you think. And if this section is too triggering or uncomfortable for you then you can skip to chapter 6 but if it hurts to read, imagine actually going through it. I believe that once we are informed on something, we can begin to be more compassionate towards it. And I'm not just talking about it for the sake of talking about it but I've dealt with being touched inappropriately and that's just one layer

I BELIEVE THAT ONCE WE ARE **INFORMED** ON SOMETHING, WE CAN BEGIN TO BE MORE **COMPASSIONATE** TOWARDS IT but there are so many other traumatic things people experience that really messes up their mind and makes them feel that they are worthless and you are not. And that's why I'm taking about this because for you to know your worth, you have to roll back the curtains and face the experiences and things stopping you from seeing yourself as the amazing person you are. I once saw something that said, "If you blame the rape victim because her clothes were provocative. You must also blame the bank that was robbed because its content were provocative." Enough is enough and we cannot continue to stand by and watch our brothers and sisters of mankind be treated like a piece of property. The great Oprah Winfrey once said in literally the best speech ever written when she received the Cecil B. deMille Award at the 2018 Golden Globes ,"What I know for sure is speaking your truth is the most powerful tool we all have." Your story is the most beautiful thing that you can share and please know that whenever you decide to share it is okay. Never feel pressured into telling your story when you are not ready. Moreover, please know that if you aren't ready that doesn't mean you don't know your worth, it just means your healing and one day you'll get there. Healing is a process and so is coming to terms with the traumatic experiences we as humans may face. Not only that, but also please understand that you have to trust yourself to know when your boundaries are being violated and everyone knows being violated isn't a good feeling. It never is and never has. But, you know what a good feeling is, knowing you did what you could to protect yourself. If I had the confidence and knowledge of my value that I have now when it happened I would've ran after the guy and might've punched him. But I didn't because in that moment there was a lot of things going on in my head. I was in utter shock. Not only was I taken aback by the disrespectful act of the boy, I had a skirt on and I felt restricted. And honestly, I wasn't strong enough in myself. I honestly didn't know how valuable I was. I honestly didn't know my worth at that time. I knew that what he did was wrong and unacceptable. But, I was afraid and wasn't sure if anyone would believe me. Now, when I told the assistant principal, her response was surprising and quite disappointing. She basically said, and I'm paraphrasing, "you should be flattered, it's a compliment, that's how boys your age flirts". When she said that I was completely taken aback and my main issue and concern was that this is grown woman was telling me this, she was supposed to be there to protect me and encourage me but she didn't. She was defending the boy and this is where we as a society fall short because of that crazy mentality. But because I know who I was even a little bit, I didn't believe that, it wasn't a compliment, it was disrespect. It is crazy and sad to me that not only did a grown woman say that someone touching me inappropriately was a sign of affection, but that many people think that way too. It' not okay and it's not true. Maybe the person does like you, but that doesn't give them the right to touch you without your permission.

Now, it happened again, and I did know who it was this time and I told someone else. And this amazing person, responded completely different. Her name is Mrs. Krazit (she was my 6th grade school guidance counselor) and she apologized and was so sorry that I went through that. She also apologized for the words and the lack of action the assistant principal made. She knew it was wrong and she talked to me about the importance of knowing who I am, so I won't think it's a compliment. So, thank you Mrs. Krazit! Having someone's support and understanding really means a lot in those situations and they are very necessary. It may be uncomfortable but talk about. Before I go any further, since we are speaking about my experiences in middle school. I must show love and appreciation to three vital people that helped me not lose my mind during my years in middle school. My two P.E coaches, Coach Medley, Coach Kari, and my theater teacher Mrs. Moore. Coach Medley and Coach Kari were both devoted Christians, so they always gave me wise and Godly counsel. They were my voice of reason and they gave me some of the best guidance I have ever received in my life. Coach Kari specifically prayed with me, listened to me, wiped my tears, and held my hand through the toughest of times and I'll forever honor her for that. Another teacher that supported me and encouraged me was my theater teacher, Mrs. Rachel Moore. She was my teacher for all 3 years and she always knew when something was bringing me down and she was just the best. Just writing about her, brings tears to my eyes be-

cause although I never told her in detail what happened with the guy in 6th grade, her classroom was a safe haven for me. I cried in that class more than any class and more than anywhere, I felt safe and accepted. I love theater so much, and it was a way that I could express myself. Every student deserves that a Mrs. Moore. She was the best teacher and I looked forward everyday entering her classroom and although she changed classrooms, wherever she was, was home. Mrs. Moore was more than a teacher but she was a mom to so many of her students. I will never ever forget her and although she never said she loved her students because she felt it was inappropriate as a teacher, I knew she loved me and I still plan on sending her random checks one day. You may be thinking, that was random. But, I decided to show that appreciation to those 3 individuals because I honestly don't think I would have been the person I am today without them which would mean I wouldn't have written this book. So thank you Coach Kari, Coach Medley, and Mrs. Moore.

Now, back to what I was saying, please know that your healing redefines you from a victim to a survivor. You know, (insert your name) If I'm honest I was afraid to write about that situation and to even write about sexual harassment and things of that nature, and not because I'm ashamed, but because it's not something people want to talk about. And often times, if it is addressed, it's minimized and dismissed as if it is insignificant. They often say it's something you just have to deal with or just figure out. But you don't. Take a stand, tell someone, don't be ashamed and do your best to make sure that something is done. Those experiences are something people feel that they will be judged about or looked at weird because of. But, they shouldn't be. Those situations like those have the power to shape your identity and you shouldn't be judged because of that. If you were abused, that can drastically change the person you become and the outcome doesn't necessarily have to be a negative one. Maybe, because of what you went through, someone can relate to your situation. If they are still struggling, seeing you overcome can help them feel like they can too and if you are still overcoming they can join you on your journey. Realize that what you went through isn't your fault and you're not weird. Someone went through the same thing you went through and you are not alone.

Also, I want you to know that words can also be a weapon that hurts as well. I want you to know that sexual assault isn't just the act of someone touching or attacking without the persons consent, but verbal assault is a thing.

People's word can deeply hurt someone, and I can't just say be strong and know you're beautiful. But, know hurt people, hurt people. It has nothing to do with you, but everything to do with them. There's an amazing talk show called *The Real Daytime* and because of that show I had the guts to tell my dean about the situation. One of the talk show host Jeannie Mai went through something similar to my situation and I remember her saying something so simple but so powerful. She said, "it's not okay, no woman should have to go through that "and I remembered that statement and what she went through in my head while walking to the dean's office. She also spoke on how men or even boys can undress you with their eyes and sometimes they don't even say anything or touch you but just the way they look at you forms knots all in your stomach. Again, I know this may be uncomfortable but this is real life stuff. So, to specifically young girls, it's not cute and he's not just playing, its assault and a sign of disrespect. You have to know and understand your worth in order to stand up for yourself. Now, he might be playing, but it's still not okay. Don't be baited into the shame and stigma that often comes with those kinds of experiences. You have to know your WORTH. If you don't know your worth, you will be okay with people treating you any and anyhow. When you don't know your worth, you will give people discounts. You set the standard and don't take anything lower than that. You set the standard of how people treat you by how you treat yourself. You have to know and understand your worth for you to stand up for yourself.

Moreover, sometimes girls who aren't loved at home, especially by their father, when they see or feel or are given some type of love by another male figure they take it and try to get as much of it that they can, no matter how. And, even though your dad is physically there he might not mentally be there. So, when girls are touched inappropriately, they sometimes accept it, because they think that's what they need and that's what they're missing. But it is not. You need to know your worth so then that won't ever be okay to you. Don't be blinded and think that it is okay because it isn't. Girls and Boys never do ANYTHING you know and aren't uncomfortable doing. Again, people don't like talking about certain things because it's uncomfortable, but it's really important, don't do it, it's not worth it, that is precious, and you are precious. Do things that only align with your morals, principles, values, and your heart. If you feel alone and have connected with anything I have said in this chapter, realize that you are precious and pure and you can always email me at robynalexia@yahoo.com if you want to talk, you are not alone and never will be. Always know that if you have ever made a mistake, you can always learn and grow from it, it is never too late.

You set the standard on how people treat you and don't accept anything lower than that. Know your worth, you are not a dirty penny in the street, you are priceless. Remember a lack of boundaries invites a lack of respect. When setting boundaries, it's important to have someone there to talk to and remind you of how valuable you are and that's key. That's where those influential voices come in once again. One of the many people who help and remind me that I am valuable is my god mom, Aunty Jay. I can talk to her about anything. She is extremely uplifting and makes sure I'm not taking any and everything from people. My mommy as well, she always tells me to stick up for myself and reassures of me the importance of knowing who I am and knowing whose I am and that is the almighty God. Love you Mommy and Aunty Jay. Having someone there is so important because they will keep you on the right track of knowing your worth.

Also, remember that you should never apologize for having high standards. People who really want to be in your life will rise up to meet them. A man named Steve Maraboli once said, "I can't control your behavior; nor do I want that burden, but I will not apologize for refusing to be disrespected, be lied to, or to be mistreated. I have standards, step up or step out." Knowing your worth will ensure that you are treated in the right way and because you are the only you, you will be treated like the king and queens you are. However, even if you're not treated with respect, because of the knowledge you have of your worth, it won't bother you but encourage you to appreciate yourself even more. Remember to know your worth, you are not a piece of artwork that people can auction off. You are retail price and you better not take anything lower than that, never discount yourself so people can afford you. It's their problem if they can't afford you, if they really want you they will find the resources and money to get you. Have you ever seen Louis Vuitton go on sale? Nope, exactly.

Now, obviously you're not being paid for with money, but with time and respect. I have been in relationships where people couldn't handle me. I was too ambitious for them and that was their personal problem. And yes, I could have lowered who I was for them. But, I would and could never, that would be me putting a person's desires over mine and that's a no-no especially if it means lessening the beauty in my true self. So, in the end our relationship ended because if you find yourself being uncomfortable expressing your ideas and accomplishments with your supposed friend, that relationship will not work. You have to surround yourself with winners because when you win, it won't look like your bragging. But don't get me wrong, I was super sad when that friendship ended because we were friends since elementary school but I wasn't sad enough to sell myself short. I still genuinely care about this fellow. But you have to come to a place where you have to allow them to grow within themselves which in the example would be finding the resources to afford me and if they can't, that is not my problem. Don't let people's lack make you feel bad about you not lacking in certain areas. Because honestly, I wished that we were on the same level, so our relationship could work. But I wasn't willing to lower myself to fit in someone's small box. Never make yourself less than to fit in someone else's dream or plan or whatever it is. Know who you are and know that when you know your worth, you won't let things slide because you know what you do and do not deserve. Realize that and believe that.

But, before I end this chapter I would like to say, I am not saying if someone hits your shoulder that's sexual assault but if you are touched inappropriately and you didn't give permission that's wrong and you need to tell someone. #TIMEISSTILLANDALWAYSWILLBESUP

Knowing your worth is deeper than saying I deserve better but realizing why you deserve better and realizing how truly amazing you are just the way you are. Yes, grow and evolve but know that you are worthy of love at every stage of your journey.

chapter 6

CONFIDENCE

*Y*our energy introduces you before you even speak. *Confidence; something that every human needs to have to conquer this amazing thing called life.* A confident person doesn't need to say they are confident, their attitude and energy already does that for them. You must know that you are good enough, smart enough, beautiful enough, and strong enough. Confidence isn't a team sport it all comes down to you. Believe you are amazing and never let insecurities run your life.

Growing up, I always had confidence because I realized that I am the only me I've ever known and I'm the only me there will ever be. That knowledge alone stirs something up inside of me that just makes me love myself so much. Now, don't get me wrong like I said in past chapters I compared myself to others but I still was confident in the beauty I had within. Confidence is something on the inside that will over time come out more and more, it's always there. You may not always see it or feel it, but it's always there. At times it can be hard to be confident in who you are because the world has this picture of what you should look like or be like and at times we find ourselves trying to fit in that image. But we shouldn't, because that's not who and why God created us. God created us to be our true and amazing individual selves. Embracing your true self brings out a glow that no face cream could ever bring out. Be true to who you are.

A couple weeks ago, I was at school and I had these space buns in my hair. A boy was like, "can I tell you my opinion on your hair?" I was like, " sure." He responded, " I do not want to offend you." I was like, " You won't I know my hair is cute so your words won't offend me." And surprisingly, he walked away. True confidence is when you get to the place where you love yourself so fiercely that other's opinion will not matter. I promise you, you will get there, I was not always THAT confident. The old me would have probably cried because people's opinions WERE that important to me. I really wanted people to like me and honestly, I still do, but I am a work in progress. I think, especially because I have always been the youngest everywhere I was, I always wanted the older kids to like me. But I got to the place where it was just exhausting, and I truly wasn't happy or confident with them liking me or not. I realized even when did they like me I wasn't truly happy so what was I really longing for? Approval and when your confident you won't need that to be the truest version of yourself. So, I began to truly like me and everything about me, even the things that I thought were my flaws. I wasn't truly confident because I didn't know who I was. I realized that I could never be comfortable in who I was until I myself approved and was happy with who I was. Not only that, but I honetsly wasn't praying as I should've when I was in my lowest moments of confidence, and that's what really opened my eyes and gave me the confidence that I have today. You have to learn your habits and think what was I doing and not doing when I felt the least confident and that was the first step for me. I realized that I wasn't praying and until I started doing that I wouldv'e never been my true most confident self.

Prayer. You will find out who you are and whose you are in prayer. Because of prayer, I am more confident than ever. When speaking to God, I found my confidence. I learned that he's made you and I beautifully and fearfully. And you know, the opposite of confidence is uncertainity or distrust. So, when not only praying but when reading the scriptures of the Bible. I have found the importance of being confident in God and I have seen the countless times where he has told us to be confident in him and in who he has created/ called us to be. In Joshua 1 verse 9, it states, "Have I not commanded you? Be strong and courageous. Do not be afraid; do not be discouraged, for the Lord your God will be with you wherever you go." This scripture may have been drieted to Joshua but can also be geared to us to remember that God is with you and we have to trust in him and know that he created us in confidence knowing that we would be confident in ourselves to fulfill our purpose on this planet. So, know that confidence begins in confidence in knowing who and whose you are. Not just that but for me personally, praying and reading the word of God. Remember what you put in is what will come out, if you fill up your heart with things of encouragement and love that is what will be produced from you. And vice versa if you digest things of hate that is what you will produce. Confidence is like a tree, I feel that you have to continue to water it for it to continue to grow and even if others doesn't applaud you for watering it, still keep doing it because it's your tree.

Mrs. Adrienne Houghton said something so powerful on her talk show *The Real*. She said, "it seems like in society we are almost told to be humble to a fault, to put yourself down." And she was talking about how if you are confident no one applauds you for being confident. But when you're down people want to help you, which is great, but it's like they would rather see you not confident than confident. But, you know what I learned is that the great thing about being confident is that you don't need applause to continue to be confident, it is nice but not needed, just like the tree analogy I just gave. But, you know the other crazy beautiful thing is that when you are confident it is easier for you to compliment other people, because you already have so much love for yourself, giving it out isn't new because you give it to yourself all the time. Also, another reason it is easier for confident people to compliment others is because they know that shining a light on someone else doesn't make them shine any less and that's powerful. It's powerful because I think that's why people don't compliment other people as much, because it makes them feel insignificant, but that's not true. You don't become less signifcant because your showing love, it honestly makes you even more of a beautiful and signifcant person because many don't show love which is sad. Showing love to others is beautiful and should be celebrated.

I believe that there is a thin line between confidence and arrogance and that line is called *humility*. Confidence smiles and arrogance smirks. Please know, that there is nothing wrong with having confidence. I highly dislike when people mistake showing confidence and loving yourself for being cocky or full of yourself. But no, I just love myself. I once watched a video with Wendy Williams interviewing Keke Palmer. Keke was talking about a conversation she had with Ice Cube when she was younger. Ice Cube told her, "You need to be aware of what it is you are and who you are, so people can't exploit you "and that goes in with knowing your worth again. When you are unsure of who you are and not confident in who you are it is easy for people to use and be unkind to you because you don't know what it is you deserve. For example, if I was called ugly and I wasn't confident that I was extremely beautiful, I wouldn't respond to that person with confidence because I'm not confident that I am beautiful. But since I am confident that I am beautiful, I can respond with confidence and say, "Whatever, you thought your words would affect me, but they don't, and you failed." Know without a doubt you are beautiful.

Get up right now with this book in your hand and go look in a mirror and tell yourself, I am confident, and I am beautiful and if you're a guy say handsome." Realize that true self-confidence is the ability to feel beautiful without needing someone to tell you. I've had insecurities growing up whether it was my hair, my weight, my teeth, or even my toes. It at times can be easy to find flaws about ourselves, but you must realize that you're beautiful just the way you are, even with those small things you don't like about yourself, all of you is beautiful. But don't get me wrong, you are going to have insecurities, it's going to happen. So, don't beat yourself up about it, it's a human thing, you are not weird. Realize that people all over the world sometimes pick at their flaws and you're not alone. But, never look at yourself in the mirror and point out things you don't like about yourself, that's unhealthy. I did that and it made me feel even worse than I already felt. Don't allow those insecurities to stop you from loving yourself and believing that you are the only you. Nothing holds you back more than your **own** insecurities. As I said, I began to feel confident when I began to pray more. So, here is a prayer you can pray to God when facing insecurities.

"Dear God, you know I am struggling with insecurities within myself. I have a negative idea of who I am. It has been extremely challenging for me to disregard those thoughts of insecurity, but I will lean and believe in your word that I am beautifully and wonderfully made by you. I ask that you rewire my mind to love myself and to be confident in who you made me to be, in Jesus Name, Amen".

In 2014, I met one of my favorite people in the ENTIRE world, the one, the only, the legendary Kierra Sheard. When I met her it was the most exciting thing ever. I told her I wanted to be an actress and journalist and expressed all the dreams that I had in for my life. She said, "God will give you the desires of your heart." It sounds so simple but touched my soul in an unexplainable way. I honestly didn't know that until she told me. I honestly thought God just did what he did, but no God cares about us and our desires. That statement really helped me and triggered something in my brain. Her words helped me become a more confident person because now I know that God really cares about what I wanted and as long as my desires and his will aligned then I would be gucci. This knowledge gave me the confidence to know that I matter and my opinion matters. I also realized that God created us all uniquely different and he created us in his image. Therefore when we point out or hate on ourselves were hating on God's creation. Everyone has insecurities and flaws, but we are usually the only one that truly notices them. What we see as flaws are normally beautiful to others. You might think you have a terribly big nose and then someone else may have a small nose which they hate. So then we have a big nose person wishing they had a small nose and the small nose person wishing they had a big nose. This is why you should just love you for you. It's like that well-known quote, "one man's trash is another man's treasure." And you know the whole nose analogy brings up another point. Why does the word big have a negative connotation and small have a positive connotation? Growing up I have always been called a big girl and honestly it was always looked as a bad thing. I feel that society has made us believe that big is bad and small is good and that's not true. We are all good and amazing, and unless you are obese

Confidence 127

or even emaciated (which means dangerously skinny) then you should be left alone. And even then, unless you're a doctor then keep your opinion to yourself. I am a proud big girl and I love everything about it. Big girls aren't better than small girls or vice versa, we are all just beautiful and amazing. Moreover, this is why I love the artist. Lizzo!, because she was the first big and confident girl that I ever saw on mainstream that was confident and genuine, and no I don't support all that she does. But, I love her liberation and the unfailing confidence she exudes. Be proud and confident with who you are, at any size. Body image is such an important issue that I love that is being addressed in our society. Be confident when you're working out and be confident when you forget to workout one day. You are human, just like everyone else. Be confident in all of who you are and that includes your body. DROP MIC!

Realize that we are all custom-made pieces and most custom-made pieces might have a little thread hanging, but the fact alone that your custom made overshadows that little thread. Your amazing personality overshadows any flaw that you think you might have. That's why having a confident and positive personality is so important, because if you have a confident personality people will not just focus on what you look like but they will pay attention to that awesome presence. But, that doesn't mean don't wash your face and be a clean person because your nice, but being kind is just as important.

In Japan broken pieces are often repaired with gold. The flaw is seen as a unique piece of the object's history which adds to its beauty. Realize that your flaws and scars show your history and your past. It's proof that you made it. Once you've accepted your flaws no one can use them against you because you've already dealt with them and your already confident in who you are. It's like if I got cut by a knife while cooking and I was in pain for a couple days and the cut finally heals. The scar is probably going to stay for a while, but the pain is gone and that's the same for our insecurities. I believe life works in seasons. There are seasons of growth, pain, problems with health, deaths, and prosperities. So, if I was insecure with my nose and I finally stopped finding that as a flaw, but I loved it because it made me, me. If someone tries to make fun of my nose it won't hurt me, it will maybe bring back the memory, but it won't hurt because I have passed that stage in life and like that scar it'll bring back the memory, but not the pain.

 Now when I say flaws I am not talking about cursing people out, being rude, not using manners, bad attitudes, or anything else like that. Those aren't flaws those are bad choices you make that you have an opportunity to change and be better. Flaws are only things you don't like about yourself. But before we continue, I want you to know that there is a huge distinction between character flaws and physical flaws. Character flaws are for example, being vulgar, being rude, not using manners, being malicious, having a bad attitude, being extremely negative, and

BE CONFIDENT IN WHO YOU ARE AND DON'T TRY TO FIT INSIDE AN IMAGE THAT **SOCIETY** HAS MADE FOR YOU THAT ISN'T FOR YOU.

altogether rude. Now, physical flaws are things that are on your physical body that you personally don't like. However, only you should identify your physical flaws. But your identification should be for the betterment and not the detriment of your self-worth. People might label something as a physical flaw, but if it's not coming from the person then it's just their unsolicited opinion. Physical flaws should only come from the person to themselves not from a person to another person. But, I am not a supporter of self-criticism, unless its constructive self- criticism. For example, I was talking to my brother in law (Javaun/Lindy) and we were talking about the meaning of flaws. Lindy's definition of flaws is, " Things you were born with that you can't control. " I jokingly said like your nose (because his nose is larger than some)?" And he asked, " What if I don't have a problem with my nose? " Which brought out a very solid point.

So, since then, my definition of flaws has changed. I now think of physical flaws as things that you are physically born with that you do not like. Because I might think his nose is a flaw, but he is fine with his nose, so my opinion honestly doesn't matter. A flaw is more of an internal thing than an external thing. So, if he doesn't see his nose a flaw, it's not a flaw. Ultimately realize, that for you to be conifdent you have to love EVERYTHING about you and love doesn't mean don't change in the areas you could improve but love yourself on that journey of changing.

Positivity is a choice and so is Confidence. No, you will not just wake up being confident, but you can wake up telling yourself you're beautiful and actually believe it. When you are confident, you get to the place where you can compliment yourself. You won't need people's compliments because you have yourself. Now, I am not saying become isolated and stuck up and say, "I know", when people say nice things to you. But, I am saying be confident and happy with who you are whether or not you receive a compliment. Also, another thing just because your parents do or did something doesn't mean you have to do the same. If your parents or the family around you weren't confident that doesn't mean you have to succomb to that. Be the change you want to see. Be confident in who you are and don't try to fit inside an image that society has made for you that isn't for you. Believe in yourself, be courageous, be the best you there ever was. Because you are the only you there ever will be. Whenever you find yourself doubting how far you have come remember everything you have faced, all the battles you have won and all the fears you have overcome. Realize that you are capable of doing and accomplishing so much. A bird sitting on a tree is never afraid of the tree branch from breaking because it's trust isn't in the branch, but in its wings. Believe in yourself. Believe that you are amazing because you are. When I was younger, I didn't truly believe that my milk chocolate skin was beautiful. My mom is way lighter than me, so I always wanted to be her skin tone. I think that is a main reason I didn't like my skin because my mom didn't have my complexion. Growing up most girls want to be just like their mom and that can include their skin. But, what's important and what helped me was the fact that my mom always complimented my skin. She is very supportive in all that I do and reassured me that my skin was beautiful just the way it was. And even if you don't have that type of mom just know that your skin is beautiful. You are beautiful exactly the way you are. I remember hearing of stories of girls being told that, "you're pretty for a dark skinned girl." That would not just make me sad, but it would make me so angry because it just sounds so dumb. I realized, we are all beautifully and wonderfully made whether you're white, brown, light skin or even yellow. You should feel confident with whatever skin tone you have because it's beautiful. Now, in this pre-set moment I know without a doubt that I am a chocolate queen and people like my sisters and Gratsi, Kelly Rowland, Naomi Campbell, Ryan Destiny, Viola Davis, Keke Palmer, Kyanna Simone and so many other women that inspire me and show me that I don't have to be light skin

"

BELIEVE IN YOURSELF, BE COURAGEOUS, BE THE BEST YOU THERE EVER WAS. BECAUSE YOU ARE THE ONLY YOU THERE EVER WILL BE.

"

chapter 7

Love Yourself

Don't feel guilty for doing what's best for you. Before I talk about the basics of loving yourself. I feel that people, surprisingly mainly women, make other women feel bad about loving and celebrating themselves and that definitely shouldn't be the case. Women should support other women and men should support other men and men should support other women and women should support other men. We should all support each other. Never make anyone feel bad for openly loving themselves. Whether it's if you see them take a selfie or they say they look cute on Instagram or if you hear them saying that they're beautiful out loud. Those are things that should be celebrated not discriminated. Okay now that I got that off my chest, let's go back to the top.

Loving yourself, what is truly loving yourself? People say this statement all the time, I mean Justin Bieber has a song entitled this. But what is truly loving yourself? Do we truly know what it means and how to do it? Loving yourself for me, is when you unapologetically love everything about you. It means having self-respect and unconditional self-acceptance. Needless to say, it does not mean being arrogant, conceited, or thinking that you are better than anyone else. It means having a healthy regard for yourself, pretty much knowing that you are a worthy human being. When you think about it, loving yourself is super important, well honestly, you're stuck with yourself forever. I can't move out of myself, you can with a house or your parents but not yourself. You are stuck. You will be spending the rest of your life with you so might as well enjoy your own company. Loving yourself is when you have self-respect, you know what you deserve and you're confident in who you are. Loving yourself is finding peace within ourselves and being happy with who we are.

For me when loving myself, I had to first forgive myself, and you might have to, too. Forgive yourself, for not standing up for yourself. Forgive yourself for not putting yourself first. Forgive yourself, for lying to yourself, and forgive yourself for saying and doing something you know you shouldn't have done. But at the same to my love, relax. I know that was a lot of things to forgive yourself for. And yes, do all those things, but don't be so hard on yourself. Daily we are living and growing. Forgive

REALIZE THAT DWELLING ON PAST DECISIONS YOU'VE MADE WILL ONLY ALLOW THOSE DECISIONS TO KEEP DEFINING YOU

yourself and learn from the experience. Realize that dwelling on past decisions you've made will only allow those decisions to keep defining you. Rihanna once said, "the minute you learn to love yourself you won't want to be anyone else." I promise that is so true. Once you truly dig deep down into yourself and find out who you truly are you will not want to be anyone else but yourself. Fighting to be yourself, in a world that praises being someone other than yourself is the most important fight of your life. Don't ever throw in the towel. Loving yourself truly means to love yourself fully.

We must all realize and come to the place that we accept we are all going to make dumb mistakes. However, those mistakes shouldn't make you stop loving you and they don't define you either. And I am not saying purposely make mistakes because you love yourself but know that even when you make those mistakes you are still lovable and you should be the first one showing yourself all the grace and love that you show when others make those same mistakes. I feel that we show so much love and grace to people when there down and not enough to ourself and that is the first thing I want you to do. Show more compassion and empathy to yourself.

Now, another thing I want you to know, is for you to truly love yourself, you have to be confident in who you are. In most cases, when you love someone you have gained trust and confidence towards that person and that's the same for yourself. You have to be confident in oneself to truly love yourself. Loving yourself is when you truly know what makes you happy. When you love another person, you get to know that other person. Well, that's how you should treat yourself, like another person. If I were to ask you, what things do you do that makes you happy? I pray that you can answer that question and if you can't, you've got some work to do. Get to know yourself, find out who you truly are. Take time with yourself, if you make a mistake don't hate yourself, love you even more. I mean that's what you would do for another person right? Like I just previously said, I feel that we love others more than ourselves and I'm sorry, but I love me a lot. We treat others better than ourselves and that is wrong in my opinion. Yes, care for each other, but don't burn yourself trying to burn out somebody else's fire. They are well capable of blowing just like you and that's not to say don't lend a helping hand when needed but don't forget about yourself too.

There is this song called *I Love Me* by Meghan Trainor and it is so fun and I literally love it. My favorite part is when she says, "I don't mean to brag I don't mean to boast I love yall, but I love me the most." You should definitely listen to it, the song is super encouraging and has a great message. But love yourself, man, like you're amazing. I believe you should love you the most, you are the only one. The sad and honest thing.

Now, I believe there are many reasons of why it can be very hard at times to love ourselves, one being because we try to be perfect or at least conform to society's definition of perfection and then we fail, and then we get upset with ourselves for not being *perfect*. But, first please understand you will never ever fit society's view of perfection, you'll either be too light or too dark, or not small enough, or not curvy enough, or not talented enough, there's never a win-win in societies point of view. But, what society thinks is beautiful doesn't have to be your idea of beautiful and to be quite frank their definiton of beauty is wrong and is narrow like the minds of people who support it. You are beautiful, unique, and amazing and that's all that matters. So, stop trying to fit in other's images or perceptions of beauty. Love everything about you, because all of you was made by God and everything God touches is good. When you love yourself, it will be easier to love other people. If you find yourself struggling to love people and forgive people, maybe you don't completely and truly love yourself. Maybe you haven't forgiven yourself from that thing you did 20 years or 5 years ago, you haven't let it go, so you can't completely love yourself. If you have unresolved issues in your heart, you won't be able to completely love yourself effectively and definiely not other people.

When you have old spoiled rice, you can't put new freshly cooked rice on top of it, even though it's both white. That doesn't make the old rice, new rice all of a sudden. The longer we try to pretend it's not there, the longer all of the rice begins to spoil. That can end up happening to us if we don't admit our problems and don't honestly express how we truly feel about ourselves. For you to effectively and truly love others you **must** love yourself first. I hear the statement "fake it till you make it" all the time but is that really healthy? Not really in my opinion. Yes, you should always try to be positive because positivity is a choice. But, sometimes we get so used to "fake it till we make it", we don't know who we are anymore, and you can't love someone that you don't know or connect with. Fall in love with yourself, we must realize that falling in love with ourselves does not make you vain or selfish, but it makes you indestructible.

A woman named Anna Taylor once said something so profound. She said "love yourself enough to set boundaries, your time and energy are precious, you get to choose how you use it, you teach people how to treat you by deciding what you will and will not accept." This means that you allow people to treat you bad and you allow people to treat you good. If you don't show yourself love and respect, how do you expect others too? You show people how to treat you. It's like your bedroom. If your bedroom is a mess and full of food and junkiness, if your friends come in your room, they are going to add to the junkiness. You set the standard of how people treat you by how you treat yourself. Treat **yourself** how you want to be treated. When you truly love yourself, you will know what you deserve. You set the bar. However though, when loving yourself you also have to realize that some people might have a problem with you loving yourself, but they don't matter. You have to realize that not everyone will love you and everyone doesn't have to and because you love yourself, it won't matter because you do and that's all that matters. If you are being true to yourself and somebody has a problem with that, that is their negative energy to deal with, not yours. Loving yourself is knowing that you will never have the love, praise, and approval from everybody you meet, but you know that doesn't reflect anything about who you are.

I honestly at times struggle with that feeling that if I'm not complimented it means what I'm doing or saying isn't right or valid. I'm realizing every day that that's not true. Love yourself so much to the point that your energy and aura rejects anyone who doesn't know your worth. If you love yourself everything else will fall in line. You really have to love yourself to have a successful life. And when I say that I mean that loving yourself is vital in walking through this life with your head up. When you love yourself, you won't take foolishness from people and you won't consume foolishness and you won't become foolish, and all because of the love that you have for yourself.

A woman named Diane Von Furstenberg once said, "you're always with yourself, so you might as well enjoy the company." Loving oneself is extremely vital to our existence. You're literally with yourselves forever. Be happy with who you are, be proud of who you are, and embrace who you are. My favorite out of those 3 is embrace who are. Embrace your love for food, embrace that gap in your teeth, embrace those long legs, and embrace those small eyes. Embrace everything about yourself because you really can't do anything about yourself. Well you couldn't in the 1800s but now you can. There's this thing called plastic surgery where you either add-on or even take something off your body. Now yes you are capable of doing that, but I mean if you were supposed to have a small nose, God would've given you a small nose. Be happy with who you are. Now, let's say you do plastic surgery, now you and Rhonda (a random name for my example) have plastic in your butts and now you're even more similar. See that's why you should leave yourself alone. Also, if you do plastic surgery now, then when your face starts changing in 10 years you might look like a weird monkey, just saying. Love yourself because well why wouldn't you, you're awesome. Don't change to fit society's image of what you should be like, but create your own image because you are the only you. I challenge you, love yourself as much as

chapter 8

YOU

*H*ey you! You are beautiful, you are smart, you are a conqueror, you are capable of doing anything and everything you put your mind to. You are strong, you are ambitious, and you are going to put 100 % energy in everything you do today because you don't know if you will live to see tomorrow. This is what you must tell yourself every day to be a true self-confident person. Remind yourself how spectacular you are because if you don't how else will you be able to receive it from other people? You are literally breathing right now! What are you doing? How are you bettering yourself as a person? Do you tell yourself you are beautiful? Because you are! Do you let people's opinions change your opinion on yourself? I hope not because their opinion should be the last of your worries. You're amazing, beautiful, and confident in who God made you to be. Speaking positively will truly change your life. A positive mind equals a positive life. A negative mind equals a negative life. But, don't stress over the times you don't feel 100% and full of happiness, because you're human. We're all human and humans sometimes feel that way.

 My sister Akeima has taught me thousands of life lessons. But one of the most important ones has been; it's okay not be okay It's okay, and it's okay if you fall or don't feel that good about yourself. But, always get up and when you get up, get up stronger and fiercer than ever. Knowing that it is okay not be okay, gives you comfort and everybody loves comfort but don't get too comfortable. It's okay not to be okay for only so long. And only you can decide when its too long but you have to be honest. If you have a horrible day Wednesday, try again Thursday and have a great day Thursday. Always make today better than yesterday and if you don't it's okay, try again the next day. All you can do is try and then try, and then try another way. Donnie MCclurkin said it best in one of his songs, "we fall down, but we get up, for a saint is just a sinner who fell down and then got up." These lyrics speak so much volume because if we think about it, we are all people just tryng to make it. Not just that but it says that a saint is just a sinner who fell down but then got up, which means that the only difference between a saint and a sinner is that saints ability to come face to face with their issues and get back up. I want you to know, that you are just one step closer to the life you have always wanted . You just have to believe in yourself and know that you can make it. And not just that but know you are also one step closer to not having the life you have always wanted. All it takes is one bankrupcy or fire, or virus, or one tornado, eveyrthing can change and that is why we must remain humble and grateful. Because everything can change in an instant but who you are deep down doesn't have to change and that is what I pray you got from this book. I pray you know that who you are on the inside should be a reflection of how you act on the outside and that your character and your words have power. You are the only you, regardless of what life throws at you.

Another point I want to make is that, those celebs you see on Instagram and Snapchat. Please know that they're not always having their best day, but they usually only post their best days. Nobody posts when they look like a hot mess. They post when they look their cutest and don't lie, you do it too, and there's nothing wrong with that. People show the best version of themselves because they don't want to look bad. And I am not saying the best version of your self is when your hair is done and you look all done up but society has made it that way. But, in my opinion your best self is when you feel your best about you and your hair or makeup doesn't have to be done for you to feel that way. So, all I am really saying is that we are honestly all more similar than we like to believe. Celebrities might have more money and more people might recognize them at the mall, but we all are human, and all have feelings.

Don't ever feel less than. You don't know what that other person is going through. This is why you need to literally be in love with you because you're like OMG! THE ONLY YOU EVER. Like really think about it you are so unique, it is so crazy! And the best thing about you is that you are limited edition, so there are no other copies. Which for some people we should be glad there aren't (lol) we couldn't deal with 2 of them. You must realize that you'll never be perfect, but you will always be capable of being the best you that you can be. Every one of us is in the process of growing and that is the beauty of this thing called life.

One of the photographers for this book Katwon once said while we were talking about life during the shoot "they weren't bad experiences they were growing experiences. "Every "bad experience" you have had honestly has been a growing experience." They helped you be and become the *you*, you are today. We're always growing and we're always learning new information. But everyone's growing process is different, and you must know that you cannot become the best you by remaining to do what you normally do.

Same stuff= same results. Different stuff= different results

Madonna once said, "A lot of people are afraid to say what they want and that's why they don't get what they want." That is entirely true because if you're afraid to declare and speak in existence how you want to be and how you want your attitude to be, you will always be bound and chained up to the old and boring version of yourself. You have to be confident in the change you want to see in yourself. You cannot be timid when trying to birth the better version of yourself. Do you think pregnant women in labor just sit there? No! They get in position and push! And scream if they have to. You have to be willing to do what it takes to grow and become the next and better version of yourself. And after you push and become the next and best version of yourself, don't be afraid to congratulate yourself.

Don't ever feel ashamed of complimenting yourself. Don't be conceited and annoying and say, "like I'm the best in the world and everyone should be like me," that's annoying. But you're not conceited for looking in the mirror and saying, "I look really beautiful today or good job for overcoming that private struggle". You are so amazing and if you feel that you did a great job at something, don't be afraid to say it, even if it's just to yourself. A little progress a day leads to big results one day and that's a beautiful thing to celebrate.

Quick question: Have you ever been told you look super nice and you deep down know you look super nice and you want to say, 'I know right.' But you can't because you'll sound conceited if you do. Now don't get me wrong, I'm not telling you to say," I know right "but when you're complimented, take it and don't brush it off. When you're told something nice say "thank you so much, I really like these shoes too or that is so sweet, but don't say "don't lie to me, I look so ugly. " People don't realize that when you do that you're lowering your own self-esteem. Receive the compliment; don't put your own self down. Sometimes we say other people are putting us down, but we are the ones putting our own selves down. If I am honest, I did this a lot. I would dodge peoples compliments because I felt weird and honestly didn't receive them myself. But, now that I am confident in who I am, I receive all the compliments tastefully and show apprecation as well.

Remember, it's not what you are that's holding you back; it's what you think you are. Everything is a mind thing, everything starts in the mind. When you picked up this book, in your mind you had to think before you did it. A signal went down from your brain to your hand to tell your mind to read this book. Everything starts in the mind. Bob Marley once said, "Emancipate yourself from mental slavery. " Which is so powerful, sometimes our minds are what is holding us back to becoming our best selves. You have to free yourself from bad habits and things that weigh you down. Think about planes, there is a reason all the luggage doesn't come with you to where you sit because the plane would be unproprtional. That is why they compartmentalized it, the way they did and you too, have to do the same with your mind. You have to organize your mind and the thoughts that come into your mind. It is said a double minded man is unstable in all his ways. Do you want to be unstable? No, I thought so. So clean up your mind, it's important. Your mind controls everything. Keep these thngs in mind: If you can think it you can do it. Don't ever pull yourself down. Be your #1 fan. Don't be the one stopping yourself from being great. And lastly, Don't stand in your own way.

So quick recap:

- You have learned about your DNA, you have learned about your Individuality
- You have learned on why you should not compare yourself
- You have learned on the impact of influential voices
- You have learned about how to know your true worth
- You have learned how to be confident
- You have learned how to truly love yourself

Now YOU have to make the decision on what you are going to do with this knowledge. You are capable of being the most confident

truth is that when you leave this lovely earth, you are leaving alone. So, make it your mission to spend every moment you can, loving and living your best life. Loving yourself means that you love and appreciate your unique beauty. So what if my hair isn't as long, as Lilly Singh. So, what if I don't sing like Beyoncé. And so, what if my nose is big. You are your own kind of beautiful. You must realize that beauty doesn't come from appearance, but comes from within and everyone says but it really is true. I know we have all met some pretty people but when they open there mouth you can feel the negative energy and that's what I'm saying. Now, this doesn't mean they aren't pretty but are they beautiful? My definition of beautiful is to be shining out kindness outwardly and inwardly. Not just that, but to be beautiful means being your true unique self. You don't need to be accepted by others, you need to be accepted by you. If you don't accept you, others acceptance of you doesn't really matter.

Alicia Keys once said to a contestant WE' McDonald on *The Voice* "I don't want to be like anyone else and I don't want you to be like anyone else, you were born to show the world what love sounds like. " So, I tell you the same thing, don't desire to be like anyone else, desire to be more like you. I remember one day I washed my face like just any other morning and I looked at myself in the mirror and said to myself, "You are so beautiful, and I love you." I literally right then and there started to cry because I thought of all the times I looked at myself in that same mirror and picked out my flaws. I truly in that moment without a doubt believed that I was beautiful. Loving yourself is so important, not just because I said it but because God said it.

Psalms 139: 14 says, "I will give thanks to you because I have been so amazingly and miraculously made. Your works are miraculously, and my soul is fully aware of this." In that point David, the author of Psalms, is thanking God for making him the way he was. In the bible, there was a man named David and he was a literal hot mess. But he loved God and was confident in who God created him to be. David loved himself because he loved God. When you love God, you love yourself because God is inside of you. This clearly states that God made us amazingly and miraculously, so why wouldn't we love ourselves? If I asked who do you love, how much can I bet that you wouldn't have said your name? We love others more than ourselves and that's not right. Please know that you are not required to set yourself on fire to keep others warm and I think that's the issue, we feel obligated. Please don't get me wrong, I am all about love, giving, and compassion, but when is the line of giving drawn? I agree in dying empty but we must ask ourselves, what did we empty ourselves out to? In life, you have to follow your heart and fnd balance for yourself. So, what may be too much for me is barely anything for you and that is A-okay, we are different and that's a beautiful you ever. You don't have to try be the only you, you already are. But, how are you going to use that knowledge now and confidently use that knowledge?

A spectacular girl named Alessia Cara knows how amazing and unique she is. So, she wrote this amazing song called *Scars to Your Beautiful* and the song to me means that as a society we are scarring our beautiful by getting plastic surgeries and by harming ourselves physically, mentally and emotionally. The song is overall about self-love and self-acceptance. Not only is her voice angelic, but the lyrics are extremely powerful. The first six lyrics of the song says, "she just wants to be beautiful." We all want to be beautiful, but we fail to realize that we don't need to want to, we all are already beautiful, and you should say this to yourself every day.

Then she says a couple lines after, "cause cover girls don't cry after their face is made." This means to me, at times we are afraid to show our true emotion. We're afraid of how we will look and what people will say. And to take it further, I believe it means that we are putting on a façade that once it's on, it's socially unacceptable to be anything else and to take it off. When you cry and have on makeup it gets ruined, so she's showing the same effect. Cover girls don't cry because it ruins the image of perfection. But that's not true, tears represent strength and the ability to express your emotion which many cannot do. I promise, when you truly love yourself, you won't care, your opinion will be the first thing you care about. We feel that if we show emotion we are weak, but like I said crying is a sign of strength. It shows you are so confident in yourself, that you don't care how you look, you express how you truly feel and that's truly knowing who you are. Then Alessia says in the song, "You should know you're beautiful just the way you are, and you don't have to change a thing, the world can change it's heart." That is extremely powerful, because at times we feel that we have to change and say certain things and act a certain way for people to like us and accept us. But, you shouldn't change for people, if they're meant to be in your life, they will love you for who you are. If someone doesn't like who you are, who cares, that shouldn't affect you because that's their opinion. If someone doesn't think you are capable of doing something that shouldn't change your belief in yourself, but make you want to do it even more. When someone says I can't do something, I then want to prove them wrong and that gives me the drive to do it even more. Now, not bad stuff but only good stuff. For example, some people don't think natural black hair is beautiful and we should do something different with our hair. Now, this is a perfect example that they need to change their heart towards that opinion because we shouldn't have to change our hair for anyone and honestly even if they don't, who cares. Be confident in who you are and even if it is a dumb thing you did, at least you were dumb and confident.

My favorite line of the song is, "no better you, than the you that you are, No better life than the life we're living". That simply means to me that you are the only you. No one is better than you because it's not a competition between me and you it's a competition between me and me. You are living the life that you were created to live and all that you are is all that you need to be at this very present moment. Be at peace knowing that you don't know what your future holds, but that you know who holds your future. Like I said in previous chapters, measure your own success on your own self and by what you did yesterday, not by the girl across the street. Be happy with who you are, because you are better than who you were yesterday and that's your only competition. I define better as having more wisdom and actually using that wisdom. Because I could have gotten in trouble today but tommorow will be better because I'll have more wisdom and I'll make different choices because of what I learned from that experience. No one is better than you, somebody might be richer or healthier, but that doesn't mean better. Every one of us is capable of doing what that person you are comparing yourself to does, it just takes dedication and belief in oneself. You have to realize that whoever is trying to pull you down is already below you, so don't focus your energy on them.

Alicia Keys once said" everything you want to be, you already are and you're simply on a path of discovering it." Ships don't sink because of the water around them, but they sink because water that gets in them. Don't allow what's happening around you to get inside of you and weigh you down because then you end up drowning. Take control of the ship.

Be strong and overcome, because you can do it. Seeing others who look like you do the same thing also aids you in becoming the best you. That is called, representation and it is so important. For example, if you are a Latino, when you see a Lation as a cover girl, that makes you as a Latino or any minority honestly believe that you too can be a cover girl. But, if you only see white cover girls then you are going to think that they are the only kind of people who can achieve it. So, having representation is amazing when developing into the best you. Even me, starting to write this book at 12 years old was scary. But, maybe because of my example other 12 year olds are going to think they can do it, because they can! Identifying yourself in others who are achieving the succuess you desire gives you the belief that you can do it too. There is this amazing woman,

Love Yourself 161

Dr. Joan E. Whittaker that I absolutely love, admire, and adore and I'm extremely inspired by and I could go on and on forever about. She is a Pastor and Bishop in Ossining, New York. Women pastors and definitley not bishops weren't always accepted. People believed, and some still believe, that women aren't capable of being pastors. But, she is one of the best Pastors and Bishops I know, so there clearly wrong. She is the first women Pastor and Bishop I have ever met, and she is the kindest most loving person ever. Knowing her and seeing her do such an amazing job as a Bishop and Pastor, I now know and have an example that if I wanted to be or was called to be a pastor (which I highly doubt will happen) I could, and I would have great role model to follow. Representation matters and it's extremely important.

Well here we are, we've reached to the end of the book. I truly hope that what I have said has benefited you in some way. I truly want you to be confident in who you are and I want you to conquer the world in any positive way you can. Remember, there will be rain, but remember without rain there will no rainbow. And because of that rain a flower will bloom and you are that flower, so Bloom! It will all work out in the end. Dr. Seuss said it best "Why fit in when you were born to stand out." You weren't born to be like anyone and that's why we were created so differently.

Beautiful human reading this (yes, that's you). While conquering and being the best you, do it confidently and with assurance that you are amazing because you are. We were all created for a purpose, and we should all fulfill that purpose with confidence. You are what you do, not what you say you say you will do. So, after reading this you will probably say I am going to be a confident person and I'm going to love myself unconditionally, but don't JUST say it, just DO IT!

Walk with confidence, breathe with confidence, live with confidence, eat with confidence, talk with confidence, be the best you with confidence and just be the best you ever because *You* *Are The Only Ever*.

Remember, the two things that prevent you from being extremely confident are living in the past and comparing yourself to others. I did those 2 things lot, but, look at me now, I wrote a whole book about loving yourself (lol). Also remember, none of what I have told you will happen overnight. Everything is a process, don't rush it. You're like an airplane, there might be turbulence, but keep flying YOU will get to your destination.

You *Are the Only* *You* isn't just a statement or book title but it is a fact. So speak that, breathe that, and live that because You truly are the only you.

Other *Woman's* Road to
CONDFIDENCE

Oh, and my Daddy too!

Akeima Young

"Does the sun ask itself, "Am I good? Am I worthwhile? Is there enough of me?" No, it burns and it shines. Does the sun ask itself, "What does the moon think of me? How does Mars feel about me today?" No it burns, it shines." One of the keys to unlocking a deep and unshakeable self-confidence has so much to do with the wisdom in that quote by Andrea Dworkin. Self-confidence for me is an extension of a deep understanding of my purpose. Even though I have dealt with depression and the inner turmoil that comes with suicidal thoughts since I was younger, I always knew somehow that I was here to do more than experience pain. I came to a crossroads in my life when I had a choice to make between carrying out a suicide attempt that left no room for me to be saved or revived and to seek help. When things got dark and I couldn't breathe or see any way out, there was this dim light inside that allowed me to hold on and that wouldn't let the darkness take over completely. Even though I felt like I was drowning and so unsure of my strength and worth there is something inside that felt more real to me than all of the mental and emotional turmoil. That inner knowing was the thing that we are all born with it was the truth, everything that God creates has a purpose, every animal every star, every insect plays its part in this world we call home. The confidence I have now can't be taken away from me by anyone or any situation, because by the grace of God I built it from the ground up.Through falling down thousands of times and always getting back up. By learning how not to judge myself for the falls and celebrating being willing to start over, I now have faith in my ability to fight for my purpose. When I find myself in difficult situations or when I have mental battles I recognize now that I have a power from within to overcome that cannot be shaken because I was brought to life by God to accomplish something that no one else can. Just like the sun, and just like you.

Jhaneal Hector

"Homo sum, humani nihil a me alienum puto". These are the words written by Roman playwright Terentius Afer. Translated, it means, "I am human, and I think nothing of which is human is alien to me." This quote has always rung loud to my understanding as a young woman that have the capabilities to be all I can be and do all that I wish to do. The very same humanness that existed in Ruth, Mary the mother of Jesus, Mother Theresa, Rosa Parks, Maya Angelou, and the same humanness that exists in my mother, Viola Davis, Oprah, and Issa Rae, exists in me. The aforementioned women are all women in which I hold in high regard due to their tenacity and fulfillment of their God-given purpose. These amazing women in all their glory are human just like me. They women carried hurt, heartbreak, disappointments, and failures, but they also carried a confidence that in spite all of these "obstacles" they would overcome.

I am the dark-skinned sistah'. The rebellious and feisty one. Misunderstood. Confrontational. At least that's how the world has labeled me at different times throughout my life. However, it's one thing when the world labels you one way, but it's another thing when you believe it and begin to speak it to yourself. I embraced these negative thoughts. "Maybe I am too dark-skinned to be thought of as beautiful", "Maybe I am worthless", "Maybe being an Actress is an impossible dream", "and Maybe I will never be good enough in God's eyes."

I remember my worst season. I was twenty years old. Life was a daily battle of going through the motions. I was in a difficult relationship that I must confess broke me constantly. We were both too young; him trying to escape the frustrations of his life and me holding on desperately because I believed I had no true identity without him, as if being with a man validated my beauty and my worth. I was hitting a wall with school, a former A student who graduated high school with Honors was now failing at my classes. Not because they were difficult, but because I couldn't find the will power to try. I was pursuing a career I had no real interest in. I was living a secret life my family and friends could not see because just like Church I knew how to wear a façade. My spiritual life was crumbling because I didn't know how to face God in the midst of sins I would be ashamed to mention. I was at my rock bottom. This is where my confidence was born.

God began to unravel things before my eyes, he began to show me I was existing in a world and mindset below my purpose. Therefore, being at rock bottom, I drew closer to Christ. My favorite gospel song *I Am* by Kirk Franklin ministered to me daily. "I am so far from perfect, thought life was worthless until you showed me who I am, not here by mistake, no luck only grace, I'm on my way to who I am." If someone asked me how I reached a place of daily confidence I would say it is because I do the work. I say "daily" confidence because just like the Christ walk, it is a daily and continuous work. I began to fill myself with positivity. I read books and watched documentaries about women empowerment. I came face to face with my past hurts and began the process of forgiving myself and others. I began to take care of my body by exercising. I eliminated those around me who made me feel less than who I am. Most importantly, I asked God to lead me. These are all things I must continue to do in order to walk in my confidence.

 Just like a recovering alcoholic, it is a lifelong journey of recovery. On this lifelong journey of recovery from the many lies the world has told me and the many negative thoughts I told myself, I must check every thought in order to sustain a sober mind. The great Maya Angelou said, "I want to fulfill the highest potential of myself." This is my life's motto, "Through Christ, I will fulfill the highest potential of myself." I serve myself and the world no purpose in living in fear and low self-esteem. There is an estimated 7 billion people currently on this Earth and God still chose me, Jhaneal Kelli-Ann Hector, for a specific purpose. I can't let my God down. God told me I can do all things through Him, and his word is all I need.

Today, nobody or their momma can tell me I'm not gorgeous, sexy, brilliant, talented, funny, powerful and blessed. In fact, I am MAGIC! Living in my dream of being an Actress, training at my dream school, I discovered my passion for writing and producing as I produced my own series entitled *Pride Called Worth* on women living in their true Worth. My dreams are bigger than my fears, and the stories I must give the world are bigger than my doubts. I believe that if we live a life that when we open our eyes we are doing something that excites us, our purpose, it will drive our confidence. What's your super power? Where is your magic found? What has God placed a fire in your being for? Don't be afraid, go for it, I promise you'll never regret it.

Donstonette Jackson (Doni)

To be totally honest I didn't have the most confidence growing up. I was always picked on for my height and for being skinny. See, I watched music videos and TV and saw what television and the world praised. I wanted to look exactly like the women who I saw on my television. It's funny because my mom forbid me from watching music videos growing up. But of course, I disobeyed like most children, but that doesn't mean it is ok. What I didn't realize that those music videos would be so detrimental to my self-image.

See I thought I had to have the big butt, big boobs, and the lighter skin with the green eyes and the curly hair oh and let's not forget be 5'5 for a guy to even look my way. After a while I did stop watching music videos because I began to realize what they were doing to me mentally. I was only trying to look like what I saw. But then, I realized all the positive and beautiful things my family and church family would say to me growing up like how pretty I was and how I had such long beautiful legs (lol). It's funny because what other kids used to pick on me about, the people I loved and even strangers praised me about.

What I'm trying to say is what someone else may not like about you someone else may love. You cannot base your confidence on others. Your confidence comes from within. That's why the key is self-love first, you must love yourself. This is very essential, you cannot have confidence without self-love. Because that "confidence" will turn into doubt every time if someone was to question your ability to do something or if it's just saying you look horrible today. Even if that person was joking, you will always question yourself. Remember the key to confidence in oneself is to always love yourself.

Tiffany James (Aunty Tiffy)

You are the summation of the experiences that you have encountered. The real you is buried deep inside untapped and undeveloped until God uses the tool of life and time to mature your beauty grace and character into shape. Time is your friend not your enemy. The more we understand it the less pressure we put on ourselves and the more we cultivate an environment of peace that allows us to grow. You are not running out of time. You have to trust the God that created you and know in time I will be everything that I am created to be.

With that thought, at some point you have to make a decision in your mind that you are convinced that everything in your life is intentionally placed there. The bitter and the sweet, the laughs and the cries. At first you just feel the emotion of the moment, but maturity gives you hindsight to see life from a different perspective. My parents were intentional. Seeing a strong Mom pave the way for me. She never hid her challenges, but she showed me how to embrace them and create something positive out of the experience

. Seeing a praying father of faith that tells me prayer and faith are not the job of a woman, but the strength of a man. The priest leads his home from the guidance of a God that encapsulates all his challenges and transform them into courage. For you my friend, who may not have the same experience, you may not know your father or mother; you might have been born under trying circumstances; you are no less loved or cared for by God. Know that God was intentional with your DNA and also with the perspectives that will shape you. God can use a bad circumstance to produce a champion.

The truth is that life happens to everybody. God's intention is not to change life, but to transform you. Because how you deal with life will determine how you experience it. Celebrate your neighbor's experience, but focus on yours. This world has taught us how to look on other's journey to measure how well we're doing. God wants to renew your mind through this book. OWN YOUR JOURNEY. You are the only You!! I believe you don't have to be loud to be heard; you don't have to be seen to be felt; you just have to accept the person in the mirror and love them with everything. Your flaw today can become your strength tomorrow. Christ is the only champion of change in today's modern thought.

Be proud that you serve a God that knows that the only thing that lasts forever is Him. He is okay with your struggles because He can change them. His love allows us not to bury ourselves under failures and disappointments, but He will wait on you and help you to rise from any dust that has been thrown on us. Remember we are made from dirt. We are formed out of the dry dusty situations in our life. Allow Christ to breathe life into you and give you purpose. Take the pressure off and enjoy the process! I love you… but Jesus loves you more.

Jalila Waseem

When you are young, you are told "being different is good." But no one wants to stick out when they are young, your goal is to fit in with everyone else.

My road to confidence started at six years old when I was new to my elementary school. I was asked, "what are you?" When I would tell them black, the girls responses would be; "Black people don't look like you." I then began to notice how different I was. I had very light skin, and straight hair, so much different than the other girls. The darker girls bullied me for not looking like them. It was very hard to deal with this, but I realized that bullies want a reaction, they want to see you hurt.

 So, I refused to let them think that what they said affected me. I would ignore them, or say smart things back. Once they realized that what they said didn't bother me, the bullying got less and less. My mother told me that the only opinion about me that mattered was my own. Being looked at as different did not stop with my classmates, it extended to teachers as well. My best friend and I tried out for the cheer team in the 6th grade and we did not make it. We were much better than the other girls, and could not figure out why we did not make the team? The PE coach, who was one of the judges saw the disappointed look on our faces. She stopped us as we were walking home to explain. She told us that we were better than the other girls, but she picked the dark skin girls because we would make it far in life because we looked white. This broke my heart, I could not figure out why my own people would not accept my "blackness".Why was I being singled out because of the color of my skin and the texture of my hair? I did not like being different.

My transition to Middle and High School was a little better because there were more people who looked like me, I was no longer different!! Yay!! I still had girls who said I thought I was cute and self-centered, but I realized that they thought I was cute, and they had self-esteem issues. I did not have self-esteem issues, but I was very self-conscious about my shape. We as women compare ourselves to other women, and I compared myself to the girls at my school. I no longer stuck out because of my complexion, now it was because of my weight. I was super skinny, like a size 0! I hated my body. I once had a boy I liked tell me that he bet you could see my ribs if I took my shirt off. I went home and took off my shirt, and looked in the mirror and he was right- ribs sticking out. All the boys liked the shapely girls, none of the boys tried to talk to me. I wanted to gain weight so bad, looking in the mirror was not very pleasing to me. I used to wear tights under my jeans so that I would I look thicker.

My journey to college was better, and adulthood is the bomb!! I have come to realize that God has made each of us different, and that is a beautiful thing. My mom once told me that black girls are like a garden of flowers; some roses, tulips, violets, and daisies. Each flower is unique and different, and that is what makes us beautiful.

Girls have to remember that this journey called life is not always easy, but it does get better. Some days are hard, and you may want to cry, but just hang in there, I promise it will get better. I tell my daughter that one of the funniest looking creations God created is a caterpillar- it's fat, the color is not impressive, and it has prickly things on it, I personally think that they look gross. I love the saying that goes: "But just when the caterpillar says that it was over, she became a beautiful butterfly"! When the butterfly is in the cocoon, it is in complete darkness, totally unaware of the beautiful creature that it will be transformed into. And remember, no two butterflies are the same, each one is unique and different, and that is what makes it special, just like you.

Alia Akili

Psalm 37:25 "I have been young, and now am old; yet have I not seen the righteous forsaken, nor his seed begging for bread. "

The scripture above is such a great example of where I am today, and who is responsible for getting me here. At 26 I have travelled this nation singing, preaching, and proclaiming the Gospel of Jesus Christ. I have gone places I couldn't imagine. My feet have touched the soil of places and regions that are literally prayers made manifest. I have a thriving business that has impacted people from all different nationalities and backgrounds. I have victoriously overcome some of life's' greatest hurdles and obstacles. I have been brought before great men and women, and none of these things were accomplished with by my own strength.

Growing up I was teased badly. I remember calling my mother crying from the mean things kids said that hurt me. Insecurities continued over into my teenage years and tried to silence me. I knew I had a voice, I knew I was special, but I allowed fear and insecurities to temporarily hinder what God wanted to do through me. The presence of God in your life is so important. It was in His presence, with His power that the hindrances were removed, and divine destiny came forth. "I have been young, and now am old; yet have I not seen the righteous forsaken, nor his seed begging for bread." (Psalm 37:25)

Everything we need can be found in Christ. Confidence, love, affirmation, assurance, direction, and more are found in Him. I truly believe that we are our best selves in his presence, and in his will. It was there that I found me. It was there that I found the confidence to be me. It was there that everything I needed was made manifested. In him, in the potter's hands is where I was shaped to be the person I am today.

Sharon "Alise" Moore

My name is Sharon "Alise" Moore, but I go simply by Alise. I'm a Christian/Inspirational artist that has been singing since as long as I can remember. I am in a ministry family and have always carried the weight and responsibility of ministry. Being raised in a ministry family, caused me to grow up and mature extremely fast. I always felt ahead of my peers and that caused me to feel a bit lonely and many times out of place. I seemed to only really connect with people who were older than me.

While being mature is a great positive, it left me feeling responsible to "lead" my peers. That created a lot of pressure and effected my self-esteem. I didn't feel fully accepted for who I was but rather my value was placed in what I was able to do. I had to grow to understand that I was different and that there was value in that. My perspective changed and it allowed me to realize that I possessed wisdom that was beyond my age and that was simply a gift from God. That realization opened up my eyes to other areas of my life such as music.

I started singing at my grandfather's church when I was about 5 or 6. Naturally I'm very shy and so my mom would almost force me onto the stage. At about 15, I started leading worship at my father's church. I compared my voice, style, and presence to everyone else and struggled with feeling inadequate of being on stage and leading people into worship. Music was something that I was always passionate about and I knew that passion was ignited by God. As time went on, I began seeing the beauty in the uniqueness of my gift. God allowed me to see that even though I wasn't like everyone else, I offered something so beautiful that couldn't be duplicated by anyone else. I had to be patient with myself and give myself the grace to grow and evolve into the rare flower that I really was, but wasn't aware of yet.

Confidence comes once you can appreciate a thing. My confidence blossomed once I grew in appreciation of my voice, style, and who I was at the core. Confidence is a journey. It's not always a fast journey, but it takes time and patience. You will have days when you feel like life would be better without you in it, but those days you must remind yourself of the uniqueness of your presence. Even though you may not see your value, God found you precious enough to where no one else could duplicate who you are. Think about it, even the quirky things about you, nobody else can do those weird, awkward and clumsy things like you. Your brain, your ways, your looks are unlike anything else in the world and it's perfect. I have now been privileged to sing and perform in front of thousands of people, but I'm still on my road to confidence. My confidence has never been placed in accomplishments but rather my ability to see myself and love what I see.

Peace & Love, Alise

Jasmine Chanelle

When people see me today, they often comment on my boldness and ability to confidently share my voice as a speaker on stage, as a mentor and coach in my business, and as an influencer online, but it wasn't always that way. My journey to confidence started rocky like most young Black girls, trying to find my place in the world as a girl with kinky hair, small stature and big dreams.

All of these things made up my identity, but they didn't exactly make me confident to walk out into the world with my head held high. As a child our confidence is often influenced by our environment, as teens it's shaped by our peers, and as young adults our confidence is usually built on our accomplishments. But often it's not until we reach adulthood that we realize confidence must start with only us, and the reflection we see in the mirror.

If I could go back and encourage my younger self, I would share this advice on building confidence:

First, you have to see yourself as God sees you. You can't view yourself based on past or current circumstances. You must see yourself through His eyes. That's the only way to fall in love with you, flaws and all. The easiest way to do this is to read His word. God shares with us through scripture how magnificent we are and reveals His purpose for our lives. When you have this in mind, moving in confidence becomes second nature.

Next, confidence comes from competence, so in order to be confident in a certain area of life, you must become skilled at it. Building competence comes from repetition and practice. You have to put in the time and energy to gain the confidence you seek over time.

Finally, confidence comes from recognizing that your unique story and gifts and talents are valuable. Those experiences that you had in life are not necessarily for you, but for the benefit of you learning and growing so that you can walk in purpose and serve others. When you push past the fear that you have around sharing your value with the world you can be confident and walk in purpose.

Alex Fail

I was born into a full house of kids and it just so happens that I wasn't the youngest or the eldest, I was somewhere in between. And I ended up feeling that way the majority of my young life. I was lost in the middle, never really knowing my place. So, I began trying to fill that God sized hole in my heart with earthly things. And I failed time and time again. Unfortunately, I had to fall harder before I went to the farther. I took ownership of every mistake I made and I allowed myself to be labeled. And honestly, I didn't care to change because it would've been too inconvenient for me at the time.

I allowed men to define me and self-love was a foreign concept. Everything I learned about what a dad was supposed to be, was from television because my dad was thousands of miles away fighting for everyone else but me- so it seemed. I felt so small compared to everyone else in this big world. So. junior year I didn't think twice when I picked up a knife and told myself that it wasn't worth it anymore. I felt that I wasn't worth it anymore. And I could've died. But clearly God wasn't done with me yet because I ended up meeting a girl. Just as depressed as me. She had less knowledge of God than I, but her hunger for him inspired me. So, we started going to church together. Soon it became an obsession to me. I wanted to know how such an awesome being could exist. I wanted to feel him like everyone else said they did. And one day it happened.

I'll never forget the way my life was changed. It was like as soon as I discovered more about God and who he was, I discovered myself too. I began to fall in love with my imperfections and smile in the mirror. I laughed and smiled genuinely for the first time in forever and it felt so good to be alive. And I'm not going to lie. My life got even harder after I formed a relationship with God and it still isn't easy now. But I'll tell you this. I don't feel hopeless anymore. Because I know that even when I hardly make it through today, I know who holds my tomorrow.

Alyssia Diaz

I believe the road to confidence is directly linked to your personal journey to happiness. As a young adult, I have learned that life comes at you fast. One day everything can be perfect and then next day can take you on a complete 180 (emotionally, physically, and/or spiritually). If I have learned anything on the road to the woman I am today and will continue to be, it's that in order to exude confidence and positivity, one must be very intentional with their happiness. To "be intentional with your happiness" one must (yes, MUST) wake up every day and tell themselves, "I am choosing happiness today."One must do this, one must believe it, and one must stick to it. I do this every day to be intentional with my happiness. By being intentional with my happiness, I am forced to see the positives in a day that could've been bad.

To do this a person should surround themselves with the things, the places, and the people that make them happy. Do you love quotes? Write down some quotes and keep them in a tiny notebook that you take wherever you go. Do you love art? Create. Make something that exudes the happiness you wish to achieve. What is your favorite thing to eat? Eat that. Most importantly, love yourself. Put on that outfit you love. Wear those comfortable shoes. Look at yourself and say you love yourself. Practice being intentional with your happiness and then it will come naturally. Soon you will do the things you love because it is habit. Soon you will wake up with the intention of choosing happiness because that is what is natural to you.

Once I was continuously intentional with my happiness, the confidence fell into place. And when I have off days (because do I and that is okay), I allow myself to feel those emotions, but know when it is time to be intentional with my happiness again. This isn't about suppressing anything or holding back, it is about allowing myself to be the human I am, but being intentional about being the happiest version of myself that I can be. This has been what has worked for me. If you need help, seek it. At some point, everything will fall into place, I promise. Most importantly, I do not give up on myself because I am all I have. So, what have I done to get to this point? I make sure to never forget to choose happiness when I wake up in the morning. "

Janice Johnson (Aunty Jay)

When did I truly find my confidence? Well for me, when I was a young girl, I was seriously physically, emotionally and verbally abused by my father. It really affected me growing up and then to put the icing on the cake, I did not know my mother until I was 18 years old. So here is my dad, who was really angry because his mother gave him away when he was younger, and his father had nothing to do with him. My dad never went to school because he was working before the age of 10. He did not know how to read or write therefore he was illiterate. But now has children of his own. He did not know how to be father and he made a whole lot of mistakes.

I was the only child out all of his children that grew with him, the others were with their moms or other guardians. So, from an early age, I had to learn how to fight for myself and you know kids can be really cruel. Growing up at school I was always teased about my nose, they said that I had a big nose. I remember going home to use the clothes pins we used to hang clothes to dry to make my nose look narrower. I was so ashamed, I would try anything to change it. But the one thing that I had going for me, was that I knew how to fight. I mean I had to because of the constant abuse of my father. He would use any and anything to hit me and kick me. He used bricks, hangers, anything in his reach, so I had to know how to fight.

Growing up I never heard my dad said he loved me or a mom say she loved me. Now mind you, I did have a stepmom, but she was also being verbally and physically abused. I had no one to help me. I was alone. But what I did have was church. One thing that my step mom did do for me was grow me in church. I was going to church from the age of three. I loved Sunday School. Going to church was my saving grace. It took me away and let me stop thinking about the abuse at home. I learned to pray at Sunday School. I began to cry out to God and asked him to make me a good little girl and to make me beautiful. I did everything to try to make my nose get straight, but everything else was good. I had nice hair, nice features, but my nose made me not feel beautiful. I felt ugly, I felt that when people looked me all they saw was my nose.

But when I began to get older, people started to compliment me and told me that I was beautiful. But where my true confidence came in wasn't from those compliments. But was from me giving my life to Christ, through salvation. I turned my life to Jesus in an Apostolic Church in Jamaica at the age of 18. I was saved, and prophets and different people would just speak in my life and tell me that I am great, and I had a calling on my life.

So, my true confidence came from honestly the holy spirit. I developed a really great prayer life with God. And God and I would communicate on such an intimate level. So. while our relationship grew I started to look at myself differently, and I saw his beauty shine through me and I began not to see my nose anymore, but I began to see my entire me. Then looking past all of that allowed me to look deeper in and that's another thing that God does. He deals with the inside and he allows you to always look on the inside. So, I began to look on the inside and I realized that he has blessed me to be a kind, loving, caring and compassionate girl who loves to help people. So, God allowed me to take the focus off the outward but now the inward. So that allowed me to gain a lot more confidence in me and not pay the most attention to the outward but more on the inward.

Moreover, being active in church and truly having a relationship with Christ really shaped me into the confident woman I am. I believe that having someone speak into you is very important. For me it was this lady Iylene Williams. She spoke into my life and told me that I was called for greatness and that I should be confident in who I AM.

So, what I want to say to you is that it might not have been your nose it can be anything. But I can let you know is that true confidence comes from Christ Jesus because even if you're not saved and you had parents who validate and tell you, you have greatness and you are worth something, but it gets you thus far. It's really great but if you have that and Christ Jesus in your life, My GOD it's amazing! So, for me I did not have the mom or the dad or a family member. But I did have the church and the people who helped me and Christ Jesus. I got my true confidence knowing that the Lord said, "I will beautify the meek with salvation." I now know that I am beautiful without a doubt. I hope this blessed you and change your world for the better.

Lashonda Samuel

First off, I'd like to start by saying how amazing Robyn is. Like, she is unreal. It's funny how she asked me to write a piece for her book because she thinks that I'm this amazing, confident woman and how she admires me, when she's the true inspiration. A twelve-year-old author? Honestly, I want to be Robyn Young when I grow up. Go, Bobbie!

Okay, back to the assignment…I am the confident woman I am today because of the people that are in my life and have been in my life from a young age. I have a mother and aunts that confidently own their identity and walk so boldly in who God called them to be. Because of their example and their influence, I was able to walk in who and what God called me to be. But even though I had them guiding me, it wasn't always easy. Growing up in a world where everyone and everything wants to tell you who you're supposed to be and how you're supposed to look made it uncomfortable to be my true self at times.

 I remember when I was in middle school, which is around the time young girls' bodies begin to develop and their clothes become shorter, tighter, and more revealing, ultimately attracting the boys at school. But I came from a Christian home that preached and practiced modesty, so even though my body changed, my clothes remained the same. So, to the boys, I wasn't very desirable because when it came to me, everything was left to the imagination. One of my male schoolmates even told me that I was a waste of a good body. Those words plagued my little, immature mind for a while. I began to dislike the way I was brought up and who I was taught to be. Why couldn't I fit in? Why did my identity make me feel isolated, but also put me on display? Why was I a "waste of a good body"? It was a fight I struggled with internally because I knew my mother wasn't going to let me dress any other way, so I didn't even bother to question her.

I had to grow and realize that even though I was clothed modestly, I was beautiful. I don't need to be revealing to feel or be desired. I will attract the right person in God's time. I laugh at the fact that I even considered my classmates opinion of me, as if a good body was all I had to offer. Through this lesson I came to the knowledge that God makes no mistakes, so nothing about me happened by chance. Everything that makes me who I am, spiritually, emotionally, mentally, and physically was purposefully thought out and put together by the creator of the universe.

Truth is, on some days, I still struggle with my confidence. I listen to the lies the enemy feeds me, telling me that I'm not good enough and I never will be, but I have to remind myself that I am made in His likeness and I should find security in that identity. I am filled with gifts, potential, and I have a beautiful body. Reflecting on my 22 years of growth, I realize that it's not that I had a conflict with my identity or self-assurance, but it was the fact that being LaShonda set me apart. We have to know the difference between being set aside and set apart because confusing the two can lead to an identity crisis. Nobody likes isolation and sometimes confidently walking in your identity will lead you on a journey that others cannot follow. Be okay with that. Feeling lonely will make us believe that we need to be like, act like, think like, and look like someone else. Just know that you are no mishap. Jesus did not "runout" and just give you what was left when He was creating you. We are all one of a kind. I am the only me and you are the only you, and when you and I don't fully embrace that, the world suffers a great loss.

-Xoxo, Shondy

Kizie Quintyne- Bent

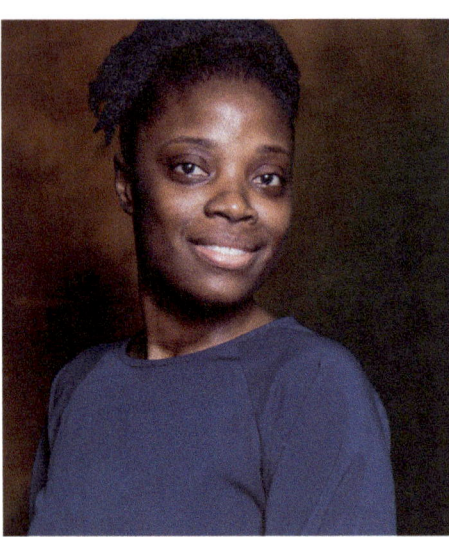

Self-confidence for me is a work in progress and my self-confidence may change from situation to situation and from person to person. Sometimes there are challenges, but I use it all as opportunities for growth. I find myself praying most times before going into a tasks or conversation that I'm not feeling confident about. And if I really feel like all could go wrong and that I don't want to lose confidence, I fast. I may even fast until I complete the tasks that I'm not confident about and it really helps to maneuver my speech accordingly and to give me the extra boost I needed in accomplishing the thing or things that were weighing heavily on my confidence.

My self-confidence also comes with preparation. The more I'm prepared, the more I invest in the thing that interests me, the more confidence I have in that area. I firmly believe that what I give myself too will give itself to me. So, preparation is key in gaining the necessary knowledge and skill set needed for me to master anything, including the leading of praise and worship.

As a praise and worship leader preparation has paid off big time. When I prepare by praying and by studying God's word and study with specific focus on the attributes of God it's always a better worship experience and these areas of preparation helps to boost my confidence and creates the drive to do more for the glory of God! Evaluating my own self also helps my confidence, I look at what I did right and/or wrong and work towards bettering myself. It's all about doing it better, but still loving myself even if things GO WRONG! I'm still learning this though, I have to say, I can really be hard on myself, but I'm learning to take things as they are, pray for the change I desire and leave it up to GOD. He knows my heart and is putting all the broken pieces of my life together. I am way too serious most times but I'm learning to shake it off and move forward.

As the saying goes LIVE, LOVE, LAUGH!! Laughter is good Medicine...Proverbs 17:22

Asking others their opinion also has significantly benefitted my self-confidence. I learn from others! There is so much knowledge out there and the experiences, perceptions, and even little chit chats with others yields a wealth of information, so I take the good or the bad and build from there. I will get sad if someone's opinion of me is different from how I view myself, but I don't just dismiss it and say they're mean or they don't know what they're talking about. Even though I'm not happy hearing it, I take stock and with God's help work on improving. Seeing my improvements helps my confidence.

I also love reading affirmations and listening to affirmations on YouTube, the more positivity I open myself to the more I tend to radiate in confidence. And of course, the word of God is my greatest affirmation! Nothing increases confidence like God's word. The Bible says that the righteous is as bold as a lion.... Proverbs 28:1. How powerful is that one scripture. Hearing that creates a roar in me and great excitement and confidence. I'm not saying that I'm all there, but I'm definitely walking it through as it manifests. It's in HIM I LIVE MOVE & HAVE THE SELF CONFIDENCE I NEED. Growing from grace to grace in Jesus's name. I'm complete & Confident in Him

Dr. Joan E. Whittaker

My Road to Confidence. I grew up in a small rural mountainous community in Jamaica. My hometown had nothing more than cow pastures, small farms, and magnificent fruit trees everywhere. There was no industry, television, telephone nor any of the technological paraphernalia we use today. The population was no more than one thousand people, most of whom were related.

My mother died when I was four years old and my Aunt adopted my older sister and I. I was the last of nine children for my mother. My father was illiterate but brilliant in many ways. He remarried and lived elsewhere during my teenage years. I started school at seven years old, a fact I discovered when I was a grown woman. My community, family, extended family, friends, and the very limited exposure to an outside world groomed me to become a very shy teenage girl.

Church life was an intricate part of my upbringing. This consisted of regular attendance to church with a multitude of rules that prevented us from engaging in most sports, drinking alcohol, smoking, attending parties, going to the beach, wearing makeup, and more. I attended primary school and was one of the few who had the opportunity in my home town to attend high school. My constraints and limitations were many. High School was my saving grace, at least that's how I felt. I fell in love during my high school years and made an early decision that despite all the odds I would become someone of significance when I grow up. I know now that it was only the hands of God on my life that created opportunities that served to transform me into the confident, mature and successful woman I am today.

I was programmed to fail by my circumstances. I should have been like the many girl friends who are still stuck with their dreams. Many have not changed much; life has served them harsh blows and they have accomplished very little. I survived divorce and it taught me management and financial skills. What should have destroyed me helped to build my confidence. I survived rejection, haters, failures, and the gamut of bad things that happened to good people. I however learned the art of using lemons to make lemonade. Every disappointment made me better because I chose to use them as learning curves. My learning curves were numerous and painful. Looking back today as I counsel people I realize I made some smart moves. My smart moves were my refusal to become like the status quo; but rather to develop a value system based on the word of God. Those choices helped to make me grow and mature into the person I am today.

One of the memories that remains with me today as a learning curve season was transitioning to a new church denomination in America. I began to visit a church that was "traditional" in their belief system in America. This was a charismatic, Apostolic church that had many constraints and restraints mostly towards women. I was somewhat vocal regarding the many "man-made rules" that were pervasive in the church but at the same time a gross lack of love, unity, and affection for people.

I was shocked and appalled that believers could be that carnal. The dress code was institutionalized and followed but the "love code" was missing to a great degree. I became determined to follow the principles of the Bible and threw myself into worship, prayer, devotion to God, loving people despite their weaknesses and simply dedicating myself completely to working in one capacity or another. Some members loved me while others ostracized me. I was absolutely not perfect, but my gift made room for me. People from many churches developed great respect for me as they observe the level of professionalism I displayed as well as my Christlike lifestyle.

Suddenly after eighteen years I visited Ossining New York one night and

God spoke to me regarding teaching my family members about the love of Jesus. A church was born, and my life was never the same again. I was transitioned from being a broken woman to a leader in the middle of the mess. The learning curves were simply circumstances and situations that God placed in my life to develop my character. During my period of struggle in church my husband decided to end our marriage. He left without informing me directly. My brother in law broke the news to me that my husband would not be returning home. For many years I was unhappy at home and at church all at the same time. I oftentimes question myself to see if I am the problem. Why am I going through this? Why is God destroying me? Why do I suffer so much? I could not make ends meet. I dealt with the curve of separation by throwing myself into the things of God. I poured out everything to God. I served more, prayed more, worshipped more and loved more.

Suddenly things changed. I was promoted to become a Library Director. God sent young ladies in my life that I adopted, and I gave love where I needed love. I gave my church my time and attention where I needed time and attention. The result was fulfillment. God filled the gap in my love. Those bitter experiences made me better. I realized that life is simply a journey. It is a process of development. Those who are smart use the disappointments to build their character and reinvent themselves. It is the harsh realities in our lives that must be used as the instruments to prune us into becoming better people. As I overcame one challenge after another, I gain new confidence. Today, I give God thanks for all the people he has placed in my life who prayed for me along the way. God did it, not me.

Robert Young (Daddy)

When my 12-year-old daughter Robin decided to write a book, I thought she would dedicate it to me and her mom Erica. Little did I know I would get a cameo. I am so very proud of her. Robin has asked me to write about how I got to where I am in life, with regards to my positive self-esteem.

Self-esteem is defined by dictionary.com as, "confidence in one's own worth or abilities" or "self-respect." This basically means an individual is sure of who they are, what they believe, and what they are capable of and what they are not capable of.

At this point in my life I have a healthy dose of self-esteem. I was not always like this, as for a great portion of my life I was always a people pleaser. I did things to make people feel good, so I could feel good about myself. Looking back on my past behavior, being this way was extremely debilitating. It caused me tremendous internal turmoil and self-loathing. I would camouflage these feelings in being nice, loud or funny. I am not fully delivered, but I no longer seek to live my life to please people. I was however always confident that when I set out to do something, I knew I would accomplish it.

My self-esteem has grown because of several reasons.

1. I came to know Jesus Christ as my personal savior. Christ has shown me so much love through my struggles and failures and has let me know how much he loves me despite me. I no longer must prove myself to anyone because he loves me.

2. Pleasing God is now more important than pleasing people. I have

seen that no matter how you make others happy they cannot truly make you happy. Internal happiness or rather joy, I have found, comes through contentment, acceptance of God's amazing grace and learning how to let go and roll with the punches of life.

3. I realize that I am indeed, bright, gifted and full of potential. I no longer wait to be affirmed by others. My accomplishments in raising three wonderful children along with my wife Erica, accomplishments in church and in school, and recently graduating with my bachelor's degree are a testimony to what God has placed in me. I have sought opportunity to develop my skills in my areas of weakness and even my areas of strengths. I am a certified competent toastmaster. I have a penchant for teaching and counselling. Self-development for me is ongoing and a life-long endeavor.

4. I have overcome failure, set-backs and challenges. I just saw a quote which said, "Life is about making mistakes and learning from them." I am still learning. I have overcome my facing my fears. My fear of failure. My fear of rejection. I do this

5. I no longer doubt myself and my abilities. There were times when I did not believe in myself. Today I am very comfortable in my own skin. I rarely put down myself, I encourage myself. Earlier in my life, I did not believe that I was going to get through my situations, but God has been faithful. No challenge for me today is too great. To ensure success in my endeavors, I spend more time preparing for the next challenge and I never back down from a challenge.

6. My wife Erica is a rock. If nobody believes in me, she does. She is always there for me and has been a source of inspiration and support in my darkest moments. The challenges of our marriage have forged in her a steely life of prayer and intercession which has made her into the woman of faith and prayer she is today. Her faith and life has empowered me to be the best I can be for her and for my three daughters.

7. The support of fellow pastors and friends. I no longer live on an island of my own making, ferrying in accolades to support my single man is-

land colony. I live among others and see people like I see myself, fearfully and wonderfully made, with purpose, conviction and destiny.

At 53, I still have a lot of living left and I am more determined to become what God has called me to be. There are times when the way gets blurry, but I am undeterred in seeking to fulfill my calling of serving God, loving my family and serving humanity. I am who I am by the grace of God. I am who I am despite what I have been through.

Robin, in writing this book, has shown all of us, that age is not a barrier to success. Age is an indicator of linear human existence, but not an indicator of human spiritual maturity.

Robin has shown that you can overcome the negative innuendo of your peers and rise above the criticism of others.

Robin has shown us that with self- discipline, goal setting, and persistence , you can accomplish anything you set your heart to do.

Robin is an amazing young lady, an incredible writer, and a true humanitarian at heart. May this initial offering by this budding writer be received, read, and remonstrated upon for years to come and be an inspiration for other young men and women to rise to the challenge of their dreams and never forget the title of this book. YOU are the only You!!!

Thank You

Thank you first and foremost to God for putting the words and thoughts in my head to write this book. Thank you to my amazing family.

Thank you, Daddy, for believing me and randomly standing behind me while I write, looking at me in approval and happiness.

Thank you, Mommy for your words of encouragement and thank you for creating your own path and leaving footprints behind for me to follow, thank you for teaching me everything I know, oh and thank you for feeding me every day of all my years of my life.

Thank you Akeima (my sister), for being the best sister ever, thank you for being my friend, and thank you for believing me, thank you for just being a living and breathing example of being the best you possible. The advice you have given me is priceless.

Thank you, Martina, (my sister) for dealing with my constant calls about this book and just in general, thank you for listening to all my ideas and believing in me 1000% and never doubting me and for believing and telling me that I am capable of doing anything I put my mind to. Thank you for showing me that you can make it and you will make it. Thank you for editing this book, best editor ever!

Thank you Javaun (aka, Lindy, aka Brother in Law), for sometimes answering my calls, thank you for always being there when I need you, thank you for making my sister happy, thank you for believing in me even when I don't believe in myself and thank you for making me realize that I do not need a filter to be beautiful.

Thank you, Aunty Jay, for listening to my crazy ideas and giving me crazy ideas and just being always there and being that influential voice in my life. You truly are the best Aunty Jay.

Thank you to all my true friends and influential voices Kayla, Ryannah, Xaria, Jaelyn, Tia, Alan, Enzoe, Zimmie, Jaaqaun and so many others for not thinking this idea was crazy but believing in me and cheering me on and sometimes answering my phone calls. Thank you all for being influential voices in my life.

Thank You Katwon and Nya for taking my pictures, Shout out to "FromWithinArts" one of the best photography companies in the world and also Mr. Pvyne

Thank You other incredible photographer. The Nvked Eye is also an incredible photography company and I am so grateful that you captured so many beautiful moments.

Thank you to all the women and my dad who wrote in, Other Woman's Road to Confidence oh and my dad too. It truly meant lot, all of your stories were inspiring and overall amazing.

Thank you to all the haters, you truly have made me stronger.

Thank you everyone, who has supported me on this journey,

I LOVE YOU

www.ingramcontent.com/pod-product-compliance
Lightning Source LLC
Chambersburg PA
CBHW040314170426
43195CB00021B/2970